Cheng Man-ch'ing

Essays on Man and Culture

Cheng Man-ch'ing

Essays on Man and Culture

Translated by

MARK HENNESSY

Frog, Ltd.
Berkeley, California

Cheng Man-ch'ing: Essays on Man and Culture

Published by Frog, Ltd.
Frog, Ltd. books are distributed by
North Atlantic Books
P.O. Box 12327
Berkeley, California 94712

Cover and book design by Nancy Koerner

Library of Congress Cataloging-in-Publication Data

Cheng, Man-ch'ing
Cheng Man-ch'ing : essays on man and culture
/ translated by Mark Hennessy.
p. cm.
Translation of forty-nine essays of author's Jen wen ch'ien shuo.
Includes bibliographical references.
ISBN 1-883319-26-9
I. Hennessy, Mark. II. Cheng Man-ch'ing. Jen wen ch'ien shuo.
English. 1995. III. Title
AC150.C51794 1995
089'.951—dc20 95-3877
CIP

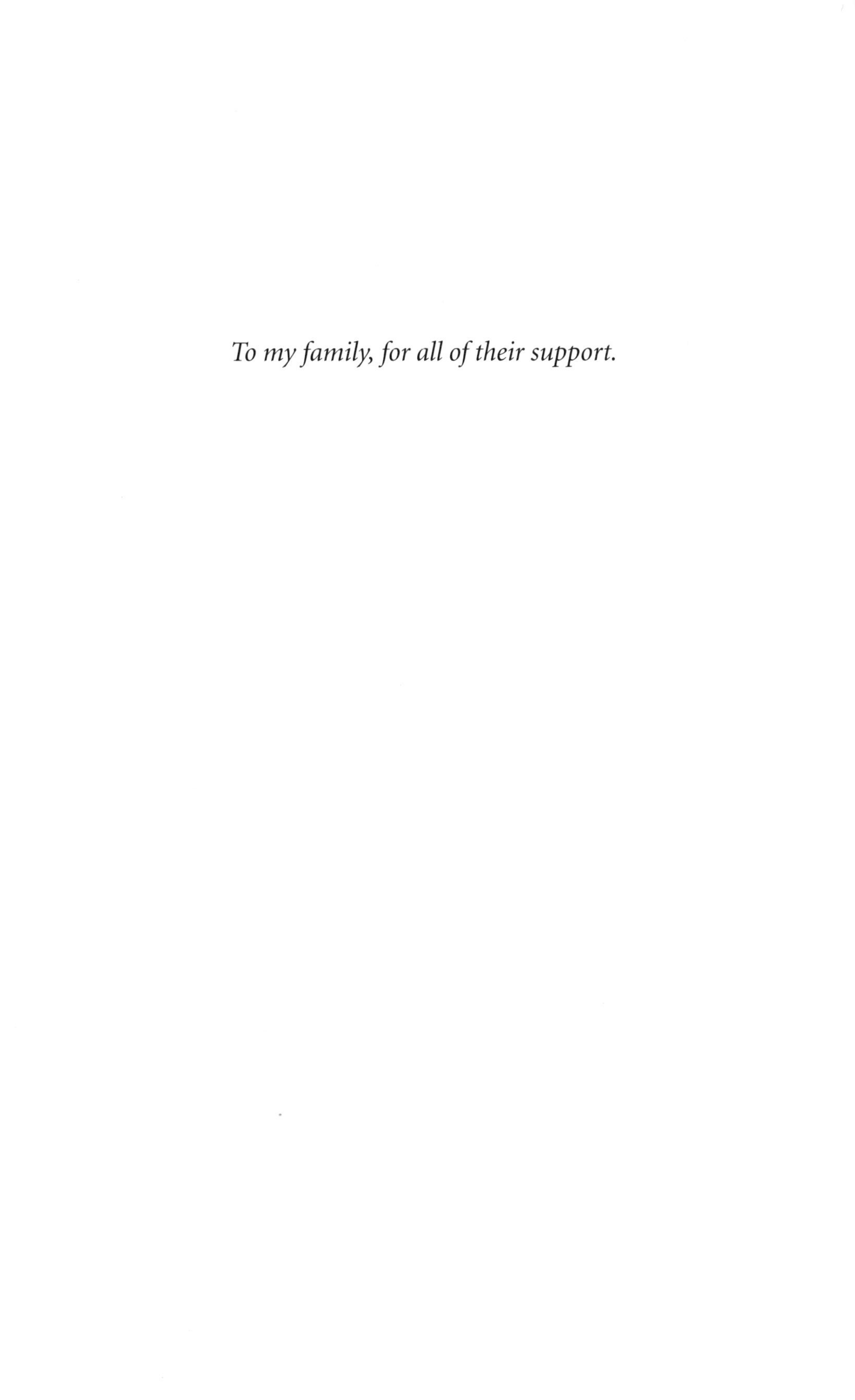

To my family, for all of their support.

Contents

Translator's Introduction . . . . *xi*

Author's Introduction . . . . *xv*

1. People and I 3
2. Vegetation 5
3. Animals 7
4. The *Jen* of Vegetation 9
5. The *Lin* and Phoenix 11
6. The Differences between Man and Organic Life 13
7. Where Organic Life Falls Inferior 15
8. Illness Enters Through the Mouth 17
9. Sleep 19
10. Taking Naps 21
11. Food and Drink 23
12. Clothing 25
13. When Sense Differs from Original Nature 27
14. Nearer By Nature 29
15. Virtuous Nature 31
16. Heaven Decrees Original Nature 33

17. Skillfully Leading People Forward 35
18. Honor Your Duty 37
19. Loyalty and Reciprocity 39
20. Conscience 41
21. *Ke Wu* 43
22. The Natural Principle 45
23. Learn as You Constantly Study 47
24. Ch'i Cultivation 49
25. To Love Virtue and Detest Evil 51
26. Right from Wrong 53
27. Revenge Hate with Equity 55
28. The Sage's Synchronicity 57
29. *Wen*, Literary Culture 59
30. Polish Your Words 61
31. Balance Substance with Refinement 63
32. Self-Completion, *Ch'eng* 65
33. Cultivate Yourself for Universal Peace 67
34. The Faults of Confucius and Yen Hui 69
35. Where Confucius and Yen Hui Found Happiness 71
36. Chung Yung 73

37. The Unifying Tao 75
38. Discerning Words 77
39. The Cultural Renaissance 79
40. Memorization through Recitation 81
41. Make Yourself Understood 83
42. Deceitful and Argumentative 85
43. Hope Versus Dreams 87
44. Fate and Heaven 89
45. Progress Daily 91
46. The Synthesis of Government with Education 93
47. Answering Advice 95
48. Make Your Will a Reality 97
49. Confucius 99

Something of Myself 101

Afterword 103

Translator's Notes 105

Translator's Introduction

Professor Cheng Man-ch'ing's *Essays on Man and Culture (Jen wen ch'ien shou)* was written in the early 1970s while the Professor lived in New York. The original calligraphic manuscripts were forwarded to Taipei, photolithographed, and privately published using traditional Chinese binding. Most of the forty-nine essays are written in the scholarly *Ching Yi* style which selects quotes from the classics as subject headings. Cheng so enjoyed this literary form that during his three years of study in the late 1920s at Master Ch'ien Ming-shan's *Ch'i Yuan* he insisted on composing these essays even against the master's advice. Undaunted, the young Cheng persevered and in the end was praised by both teacher and students. The full story is contained in his "Autobiography of a Strong Man" in my previous book *Cheng Man-ch'ing: Master of Five Excellences* (Frog, Ltd., 1995).

Though not every essay adheres to the exacting requirements of *Ching Yi* style, all are profusely garnished with quotes taken from the Confucian Canon, collectively known as the *Four Books* and the *Five Classics.* Many quotes are incomplete, some are abridged or mere allusions, and some are even misquoted—though this is common amongst scholars who have memorized the basic texts. I have endeavored to source each quote, supplement the lacunae, and correct the misquotes. The reader may then refer to the original classics at his or her leisure. My hope is not to deluge anyone with footnotes and references to Chinese classics that few people own, but rather exhibit the scope of Professor Cheng's erudition. The present work can serve as a convenient reference to the Professor's interpretation of various philosophical, ethical, and moral questions students may encounter in their related studies.

At the opening of each essay, I have translated extracts from the Professor's writings and his commentary to the classical passages he refers to or quotes from. Among the works cited are extracts from his *Analects Commentary* (1971), poetry from *Jade Well's Thatched Cottage Poetry, Vol. II* (1971), *Great Learning and Chung Yung Commentary* (1971), the *Complete I Ching* (1975), and his various works on taichi, medicine, and art.

The Professor's interpretation of classical, canonical literature is characterized by one overriding theme: a modernist return to traditionalism which interprets the classics in their relation to Humanism, *jen*—the central idea of classical Confucianism. He does not dabble in ontology, cosmology, or gnosiology. Surprisingly, apocryphal works emerging from Han Dynasty (206 B.C.–20 A.D.) cultic-Confucians, such as Wang Su's *Sayings of the Confucian School* or Yang Hsiung's *T'ai Hsuan Ching* find validity in Cheng's comments when they exhibit sound principles. While expressing the traditional Confucian scholar's perfunctory condemnation of the Buddhists and Taoists, Cheng saves his most vehement attacks for the Sung Dynasty (960–1126) Neo-Confucian, Chu Hsi, and often digresses in the middle of an essay to reiterate his condemnation of the man. The two brothers and founding fathers of Neo-Confucianism, Cheng I and Cheng Hao—collectively called Master Cheng, however, are generally praised by Cheng. One of Cheng's purposes in writing this work was his attempt to correct the mistaken commentaries of Confucian canonical literature. It must be noted that Sung interpretation of Confucianism, so-called Rationalism, has been the preferred interpretation for the past one thousand years—and continues to be taught in elementary schools throughout the Republic of China.

As a modern traditionalist, Cheng believed firmly in the monolithic nature of the classics and herein expresses only passing interest in etymology, that science which modern linguists employ to define the various strata of eras during which a classic comes into existence. He expresses admiration of the Han Dynasty books on philology and semantics but never once refers to the basic treatise of Han philology, the *Fang Yen*, in his interpretation. Cheng's commentaries reflect the viewpoint of a modern individualist/traditionalist, who chooses from the varying opinions throughout the dynasties and yet remains free from any fashion of thought, past or present.

In translating Chinese scripture, I believe in maintaining a strict metaphrastic, word-for-word approach. When these ancient quotes appear in modern prose, however, paraphrasing them is our best approach. While this allows the translator flexibility to extract the author's intention, it exposes him to criticism of his interpretation of the opus. I've been guided by Mencius' dictum: "Do not insist on one word if it injures the sentence, nor on a sentence if it hurts the paragraph." It would be highly disastrous to translate prose metaphrastically, as if such rendering is somehow more true to the original. Translating Cheng eschews a Seurat-like pointillism, where the reader connects the dots of pidgin-English prose. The Professor wrote much like the way he taught; he does not pander to the reader nor belabor a point. He will mention one subject, move on to the next, maybe return to a previous chapter's thought—and then wrap up the essay with a quote. All of this makes sense for a Chinese educated in rudimentary Confucian discussions; but for the Westerner who lacks the mesh of culture to collect such widely scattered topics, Cheng's utterances at times seem disjointed and irrational. I have attempted to collect his thoughts and place them before the Western reader in a cohesive manner.

Sadly, the Professor's scholarly works have been widely ignored by the general public and the academic world. Unassociated with an established university, he lacked the power such institutions employ for the dissemination of approved ideas. Privately published, his books lacked the resources for distribution to all but a few students and bibliophiles. The present translation hopes to rectify this situation.

In conclusion, I quote from the famous biblical scholar, Alfred Loisy (1857–1940), who spent his entire life affirming his deepest belief—that the dogmatism of the Catholic Church must change to allow for the expansion of human thought. He wrote:

> Doubtless there are some who will judge my work to be singularly inopportune in the present circumstances. The same has been said of my earlier works which were highly unwelcome to a good many people. Perhaps this work too will be equally unwelcome. Whoever has enough goodwill to see in it, before all else, a new program for the research that is needed in this field, and is far from being completed, will exactly discern the intention of its author. As for those who deem it superfluous, superficial, or preposterous, I will content myself with supposing that they themselves have not yet found leisure to consider the true character and infinite complexity of the subject under treatment.
>
> —From *Les Origins du Nouveau Testament* (1936)

We must be allowed to mold that which has molded us.

Mark Hennessy
Chicago, 1995

Author's Introduction

I returned to New York in the autumn of '72 from Taipei. As I lounged around recuperating from my long trip, I remembered that my friend Chen Li-fu said that my scholarly books were beyond most youngster's grasp, and added that, "an imposing porch discourages visitors." Such sincere advice from this seasoned diplomat prompted me to re-examine my objectives. If youngsters could not understand my writing, perhaps I am not making myself understood! Confucius always emphasized clarity and understanding.[1]

Another friend, Liu Yen-t'ao, also broached the subject with me. I told him, "The Confucian Canon is studied daily by every schoolchild, and yet you consider my writing arcane! Let's not belittle modern youth, for they can aspire to the same heights as the ancients." Liu simply shook his head. Today, while pondering these two episodes, I asked myself, "What is wrong with me? Why can't I accept their sincere advice?" I believe their point was well taken but I failed to explain myself fully. This Introduction will serve as my formal reply to their gracious advice.

I have studied Confucianism for most of life. Confucius taught that vulgar words would not travel far[2] and that you are unprepared for any discussions until you've studied the *Book of Songs*.[3] He exhorted his students to "cut, shape, refine, and polish." My disdain for unpolished prose, writing unworthy of the title "literature" is obviously not shared by my two friends. I pondered our differences for quite some time until I finally understood the impasse.

Students have been taught in *pai hua wen*, or "vernacular Chinese literature" now for more than fifty years.[4] The word "literature" cannot be serendipitously tagged on to the phrase "vernacular Chinese." Conversational Chinese is polished into literature by refining the spoken word. Chinese literature and its spoken vernacular are distinct linguistic vehicles, and if placed together as a single noun phrase, form a complete contradiction in terms. When such an irrational idea as this is promulgated as national policy, the result can only be chaos.

While a Cultural Renaissance[5] is advocated by the intellectual elite, common folk are reading classical literature in modern vernacular Chinese—is this not the "vanguard turning their swords"? Literature is an educator's most powerful tool, yet today's teachers try to impart the Tao of Confucius and Mencius with an entirely different set of instruments. This is tantamount to the barbarian tribes educating China. Our country's cultural identity is quickly regressing back to this savage level as we madly search for progress in other fields while we neglect the Tao of man.

Everyone has studied Confucius and Mencius when young, and this learning has always proven itself solid in all our endeavors. Modern youngsters are certainly as intelligent as ancient youth. Yet we cover their eyes and cork their minds, then declare them "too shallow for depth." Let us remember that their minds are as pure as unbleached silk. Need we stain them black as ink or red as blood?

This is my reply to my two friends. I trust they will see my point and support my stand. The Tao of Confucius and Mencius must first be firmly established to its rightful position in China and then used to educate the entire world. Only then can we wipe our eyes clean and await the success of the Cultural Renaissance.

These essays are my contribution to the Cultural Renaissance and I dedicate them to the youth of today, in hope they consider the Tao of Confucius and Mencius an everyday necessity—not a leisurely pursuit. We need it every second of our lives. The weight of making sure every person understands this makes me feel like I am hawking this book door-to-door. I even had to garnish my prose with punctuation marks[6] so perusers would consider it a worthwhile purchase!

Cheng Man-ch'ing
The Long Twilight House, New York
Winter Solstice, 1972

Essays on Man and Culture

I

The Master said, "I merely transmit, I do not create. I trust and enjoy the ancients. I often compare myself with Old P'eng."

Chu Hsi said, "Confucius disavowed the title 'sage' along with any attempts by his disciples to equate him with ancient men of worth. He believed that a virtuous man could transmit teachings while only a sage could truly create new principles. The fullness of his virtue is revealed in the humility of this statement. Old P'eng was a Grand Officer during the Shang Dynasty who trusted the ancients and transmitted their ideals.

"Confucius compiled the *Book of Songs* and the *Book of Documents*, arranged the *Book of Rites* and the *Book of Music*, studied the *I Ching*, and put together the *Spring and Autumn Annals*. These classics contain only the ancient transmissions with no personal interpolation by Confucius. Confucius syncretized the virtues of all previous sage-kings and selected the ideas he deemed worthy. Although in theory he merely transmitted their teachings, his achievements surpassed those of a mere compiler."

(From Professor Cheng's *Analects Commentary*, 7:1.) [All further *Analect* commentary is excerpted from this work, with my editorial changes.]

ONE

People and I

We are all members of the human race despite the dichotomy intrinsic to all men, that perception which differentiates yourself from others. Nevertheless, some people harness their talents to rise above others and not away from them.[1] This must be our goal. Do not remain second-class, for everyone is capable of self-improvement through sustained diligence.

Below I have included some perennially favorite sayings of Confucius to encourage the student:

> The Master said, "I merely transmit, I do not create. I trust and enjoy the ancients. I often compare myself with Old P'eng."[2]
>
> The Master said, "Even when I am walking with two others I have teachers from whom to study. I copy what the good one shows me and avoid what the bad one shows."[3]
>
> The Master said, "I hold no anger toward man nor any resentment toward heaven.[4] I perform my everyday affairs in a way that allows me to reach new heights. Only heaven understands me."[5]
>
> The Master said, "With no extended outlook, a man may experience immediate problems."[6]

II

The Master wrote:

"When the weather turns cold,
the evergreen is the last to shed."
Orchids scent the quiet valley,
though no man whiffs their fragrance.

Confucius is not really talking about the evergreen or the orchid, he is painting a portrait of himself. And for 2,500 years, his likeness has remained as constant, majestic, and eternal as the old pine forests. I consider this analect an example of Confucius' own poetry and have added the final phrase from an earlier source.

(*Analects Commentary*, 9:27)

TWO

Vegetation

Do vegetables have an original nature? Of course! Vegetation's original nature expresses and perfects itself by blooming. Man's nature consists of unequal propensities toward both good and evil, and so he must coordinate his latent virtue with manifest goodness. When latent virtue contacts evil behavior our nature's growth is inhibited. That is why we must perform our everyday affairs so that we grow beyond them. Then we rise above humanity just as a simple stalk rises above the field.

The Master said, "Orchids are fragrant regardless of man."[1]

The Master said, "When the weather turns cold, the evergreen is the last to shed."[2]

Tzu Yu said, "Tzu Hsia's pupils know how to sprinkle and sweep, exit and enter, or how to answer a call or respond to a question—but these are mere details. They remain ignorant of the fundamentals." When Tzu Hsia heard this he said, "Ah! Tzu Yu is mistaken. Why do the intelligent understand the noble man's Tao first, while the dullards take longer? Because people are as different as the plants and trees. Do not deceive yourself about the noble man's Way. There is an orderly progress; a beginning and an end. Only the sage possesses the Tao completely."[3]

III

Confucius and his disciples passed by two recluse scholars plowing the fields. Tzu Lu approached them asking directions to the nearest bridge. The first recluse said, "Who is your leader?" Tzu Lu replied, "Confucius."

"Then I'm sure that he already knows where it is," the recluse replied sarcastically.

Tzu Lu then asked the other recluse, who said, "The entire world is being swept away like a flood, and no man can change this. Instead of following a man who runs from one ruler to the next, why not come and join us, who have fled the world altogether?"

Tzu Lu related this story to Confucius, who said, "I cannot herd with birds and beasts. And if I am not a man amongst men, then what am I? If the world were following the Tao I would not be trying to change anything."

(*Analects*, 18:6)

THREE

Animals

Do animals have an original nature? Animals have a primal nature that relies on instinct rather than education to survive—and so their behavior exhibits no sense of morality. Whenever we breach that tenuous thread separating us from the animals, our latent animal nature can make us equally primal and irrational.[1]

> The Master said, "I cannot herd with birds and beasts. And if I am not a man amongst men, then what am I? If the world were following the Tao I would not be trying to change anything."[2]
>
> Mencius said, "Each species has one member that rises above the rest. Hoofed animals have the *Chi Lin*, winged creatures have the phoenix, and humans have their sage. Since the dawn of humanity, no one has surpassed Confucius."[3]

IV

Daily the despot Chou turned to evil. Wei Tzu remonstrated him several times to no avail, and was forced into exile. Chi Tzu was imprisoned. Pi Kan took it upon himself to rebuke the king. When his audience before the throne was completed, the king said sternly, "I have heard that a sage's heart has seven sections. Shall we take a look?" Thereupon he eviscerated Pi Kan's heart.

(Szu Ma-ch'ien, *Historical Records*)

Do not cling to the branch and ignore the root! *Jen* cultivates our virtuous nature, our root; water and fire only nourish our body, the branch. Many men have lost their lives to water and fire, but *jen* has never caused a single death.

(*Analects Commentary*, 15:34)

FOUR

The *Jen*[1] of Vegetation

Man has always attributed fruits and vegetables with a good nature because he found nourishment in them. The sage, with his inexhaustible spirit for life, emulated vegetation's own *jen*, their seeds or pits,[2] which contain their inexhaustible spirit for regeneration.

The Chinese character for *jen* comprises a "man" and the numeral "two." From its etymological origin we can equate human *jen* with egalitarianism. King Shun is revered today for his equitable distribution of the country's prosperity. Such sharing extends your innate virtue to all.[3]

> The Master said, "The man of *jen* practices nothing else. Whoever despises evil must first search for compassion. *Jen* requires work; its absence brings disgrace."[4]
>
> The Master said, "During the Yin Dynasty three men with *jen* dared to speak the truth. One was Wei Tzu, who fled the capital. One was Chi Tzu, who was imprisoned. Then there was Pi Kan, who had his heart cut out."[5]
>
> The Master said, "*Jen* is more important than fire or water. I have seen fire and water cause deaths, but never *jen*."[6]

V

The Master said, "The phoenix is gone, the river produces no map. I am finished!"

Chu Hsi said, "The phoenix is a legendary symbol. It heralded King Shun's appearance, and was spotted near Mt. Chi during King Wen's reign. The Yellow River Map appeared etched onto the back of an animal with a dragon's head and a horse's body. All these mythological creatures are auspicious omens of a sage-king's presence."

Despite their numinous characteristics, Confucius believed in these mythological omens and feared them more than any man. He believed that the *lin* was once wounded, and was worried why Duke Chou had stopped appearing in his dreams.

(*Analects Commentary*, 9:8)

FIVE

The *Lin* and Phoenix

These mythological creatures rose above the mundane animal world. When Confucius invoked their images saying, "The *lin* is wounded, the phoenix is gone," he was lamenting not only society's apathy to the Tao but his own untimely appearance.[1] Animals closest to man, like the rooster that crows at dawn and the dog who guards our home, are trusted for their assistance. Below them are animals which represent human ideals, like the orderly formation of flying geese and the amiable and loyal horse. Any man without these simple virtues is worse than an animal.

In the *Book of Songs* it is said:

> "The chirping yellow bird sits on the corner of the mound."

> The Master commented, "When it rests, it knows where to rest. Is man inferior to a little bird?"[2]

> "Lou-lou" the deer cries, nibbling on forest green.
> I have honored guests. "Lutes and zithers, begin!"
> Ah! Such splendid music.
> This vintage wine will ease our cares.[3]

人與草木禽獸異者第六章

草木之與禽獸、知其有性易、欲有以知其、
情者、未之或聞也、惟人則不同、其情易測、其、
性難言、譬猶飢者、惟思食之亟、寒者惟思衣
而務、與喜怒之態、皆形於外者、謂之情、與欲
自殺者、飢寒喜怒、皆不足以動其心者、以情不
露於外、性亦無從得而知之者也、故人之有以異

Calligraphic manuscript to Chapter Six

SIX

The Differences between Man and Organic Life

Every life form on earth has its intrinsic nature, but man alone is sentient. Plants and animals have senses that are expressed to and understood by only other members of their corresponding species. It is not man's sentience that was ever questioned but rather the composition of his nature. A starving man dreams of food; a freezing man wants warm clothes. The feelings of hunger and cold, like the emotions happiness or sorrow, are those feelings we call our sensible qualities—they are conditions "apprehensible by the senses (*sensibile*)." A depressed and suicidal person is often unmoved by his senses [his intelligent wits], and his suicidal tendencies remain unnoticed by others precisely because he may not have expressed them. In summary, the vital difference between man and other organic life lies in man's ability to apprehend and express his senses, his sentience.

Mencius, with illuminating clarity, said there is a thin line separating man from the animals. From this we extrapolate that it must be our nature, evil or virtuous, that is not altogether different from other organic life. Mencius later reinterpreted his stance and declared man's nature "entirely virtuous." This change of heart requires our careful examination.

VII

Tzu Kung asked if there was one essential word to live by everyday. The Master replied, "Reciprocity! Do not do to others what you would not like them to do to you."

If the goal of learning is to perceive the essentials, then Tzu Kung certainly succeeded in his study! Confucius chose reciprocity as the single word to carry with you your entire life because it remains relevant regardless how far you expand it—even the sage with no sense of self practices it.

(*Analects Commentary*, 15:23)

SEVEN

Where Organic Life Falls Inferior

Confucius' nature is evident when listening to the sense present in his dictum: "Do not do to others what you would not like them to do to you."[1] Confucius reached out to all men by infusing his teachings with a sense that was a pure expression of his nature. We distinguish ourselves above organic life by aligning our sentience with our nature. This unification of inner nature with external expressions is called *ch'eng*, self-completion.

The complete man bestows his virtue lovingly upon all men, shares his goodness, and finds pride in others' success as if it were his own—there is no greater virtue than this.[2] In conclusion I say: Organic life falls inferior to man, whose nature is evident through his expressions.

> Shen Nung's botanical lexicon, the *Pen Tsao*, or Lei Kung's the *Nature of Herbal Medicine*[3] show that these men attained their knowledge through personal experience, not through the Sung Confucian concept of *Ke Wu*, which is mere mental gymnastics and arcane theories, unconnected with true learning. We differ from organic life because we can base our senses upon our original nature.

VIII

The *Yellow Emperor's Classic on Internal Medicine* states, "Illness enters through the mouth," so eat at regular times and in definite amounts—and watch what you eat. The ancients said, "Never eat more meat than what is appropriate for the meal." Avoid rich, fatty, sweet, fragrant, or dry foods; stay away from foods too soft and oily—and eliminate snacks! Liquids benefit our yin aspect, so drink some liquids before going to bed and after waking up. Food benefits our yang aspect, so eat foods that help your digestion. Don't fill yourself more than seventy percent at breakfast or dinner, but enjoy your lunch and eat up to eighty percent full. We can eat more at lunch because our daily activities help us to digest the food. After dinner we are generally inactive so a large evening meal suppresses our digestive system and an illness may then slowly accumulate. Most Americans' diet goes against the Tao of proper living. A balanced diet not only strengthens our stomach and spleenic system but also prevents cancer and other illnesses.

(From Chapter 8, "Cancer Prevention," of Professor Cheng's *Eight Important Points on Cancer*)

EIGHT

Illness Enters Through the Mouth

Doctors say that the mouth spreads disease and illness enters through it; the *Book of Documents* says that from our mouths emanate both blessings and belligerency.[1] So the virtuous men remain inscrutably silent.[2] Confucius exhorted us to control our mouth when he said, "Don't stuff yourself when eating." Confucius's own eating habits were characterized thusly:

> "He liked his rice thoroughly cleaned, not spoiled by heat or humidity, and his meats fresh and finely chopped. The foods must look and smell fresh, be in season, and well prepared. He never ingested market bought wine and dried meats. He never ate more meat than what was appropriate for the meal. He was fond of ginger but not of mealtime conversation.[3]

After I finally understood these teachings I followed them meticulously—and have remained healthy ever since. Ever since I studied that the *Yellow Emperor's Classic on Internal Medicine* correlates the stomach system with the virtue of constancy, I have assiduously tried to eat only at the proper time.[4] I was discussing the benefits of proper eating habits with Wellington Ku, who said, "I always thoroughly chew my food, then 'I' maintain control." This cultivates the patience to savor your food and decreases the chances of ingesting harmful diseases. Chuang Tzu never dreamt of this method though he emphasized healthy living, while Confucius would have smiled and allowed for this interpretation of control.[5]

IX

I'd Rather

I'd rather owe sleep than take it on credit,
tonight I know I'll sleep with ease.
Greed for that sweet land of darkness,
brings me only daydreams of all forms.

Cheng Man-ch'ing
(*Jade Well's Thatched Cottage Poetry*, Vol. II)

NINE

Sleep

Confucius advised us not to sleep like a corpse nor talk in bed.[1] When you sleep like a corpse—on your back with outstretched arms—your internal organs' ch'i dissipates. Illnesses resulting from withered ch'i are generally incurable. When errant thoughts wander your mind while trying to sleep you impair your ch'i and disrupt your sleep. The healthy way to sleep is on your right side, because the right lung has an extra layer to support your weight, and curled in a fetal position that collects your ch'i. When you sleep on your left side, your heart and stomach are affected by your body weight and you'll not sleep well no matter how long you stay in bed.

Sleeping is an important part of life; we spend a third of our life in bed! Pay closer attention to how you sleep at night, for it profoundly influences what you do during the day.

X

Tsai Yu liked to take naps and Confucius scolded him saying, "Rotten wood cannot be carved, a wall of mud cannot be troweled. What use is trying to teach this man?

"I used to listen to men's words and trusted they would follow with action; now I merely listen to their words and await their actions. Tsai Yu taught me this."

(*Analects*, 5:9)

TEN

Taking Naps

Tsai Yu liked to take naps and Confucius scolded him saying, "Rotten wood cannot be carved."[1] An ancient poem says, "At dawn we rise, at dusk we rest…."[2] The darkness after sunset is a perfect time to rest—the ancients never believed in burning the midnight oil.[3] The ancients took full advantage of the sunlight as soon as dawn appeared and wondered if someone was sick when they overslept.[4] Younger and more energetic people should be especially careful not to confuse dusk with dawn nor dispute the natural principles of work and rest. There are, of course, special circumstances; Duke Chou would arise before dawn,[5] and bridled soldiers often staged night attacks.[6] But these are examples of extraordinary physical training.

If you cannot fall asleep one night, just relax the next day. Visit the forest, rest under some trees, or sit by a river. Do anything you like—but don't sleep! Climb into bed earlier that night, for there is nothing finer than a nice long sleep.

XI

Eighty to ninety percent of all illnesses come from poor eating habits—so watch what you eat! Many people injure their stomachs by ingesting high nutritional supplements when they feel weak. But this can actually cause an illness because the stomach is too weak to digest such dense nutrients. The stomach becomes suppressed, which stagnates blood circulation—which produces an illness. The best way to prevent illness is to keep your blood circulating freely, and nothing does this better than taichi.

(Lecture by Professor Cheng to the Taichi Ch'uan Research Association July 20, 1970, Taipei)

ELEVEN

Food and Drink

The *Chou Book of Rites* assigned the Imperial Chef the duty of preparing the King's food and drink.[1] Liquids such as tea, wine, and soup were to be thin and watery—this nourishes the yin/blood aspect. Solids included rice which nourish the yang/ch'i aspect. When yang/repleting ch'i is depleted, the resulting illness is curable. If the yang continues to deplete until the nature turns yin, the excretions of the internal organs dry up and the ensuing illness will be quite serious.[2]

Speaking of ch'i, Chinese medicine divides ch'i into three categories: 1) blood ch'i, 2) *ching* essence ch'i, and 3) *yuan* undifferentiated ch'i.[3] The *Pen Tsao* considers grains as the only perfectly balanced nutrition for supplementing ch'i. But Western doctors disagree. They discount the theory of supplementing ch'i with grains by citing its high starch content, and even suggest limiting our intake of grains—such is the lop-sided mentality of Western scientists. They study only the physical body and are ignorant of ch'i. True scientists would not immediately label my ideas as fantastic while blindly discussing nutrition without a serious investigation. Each of our organs requires its own peculiar nutrition and illnesses may easily develop through misguided supplementation. The idea that liquids supplement our yin aspect is not easily understood.

XII

The Master said,
"Yu was never ashamed to stand beside men dressed in furs though he himself wore cheap, tattered garments. I would describe him saying, 'He hates no one; he covets nothing. Everything he does is good.'"

Afterwards, when Yu was heard repeating these lines to himself, Confucius told him, "I did not compliment you so that you would treasure a single sentence."

(*Analects*, 9:26)

TWELVE

Clothing

Clothing has two uses, personal and social. It keeps us alive and warm during the cold seasons while it maintains social etiquette. Confucius kept warm at home by wearing fox or badger fur,[1] but a simple leather coat or cheaper fur can also keep you warm. To just cover your body, lotus leaves and a grass skirt can avoid embarrassment. But to maintain social etiquette we should emulate Emperor Yu, who wore simple clothes but owned beautiful sacrificial vestments.[2] Confucius' disciple, Chung Yu, was also unashamed wearing a tattered hemp robe when standing beside men dressed in furs.[3] The Yellow Emperor, Kings Yao and Shun, all maintained beautiful vestments and believed that by first regulating their personal habits, including their clothes, they could then extend that governing to all under heaven.[4]

During his childhood, Confucius wore the long-sleeved garment from Lu; when he was older he wore the Sung cap of manhood.[5] He believed the noble man should dress humbly not just to distinguish himself from the secular world but to suit his own humility.[6] I dress in traditional clothing because the Republic has yet to institute a dress code, so I wear what is comfortable. The importance of a dress code is to distinguish the superior from the inferior and to maintain appearance. It is an important aspect for governing officials.

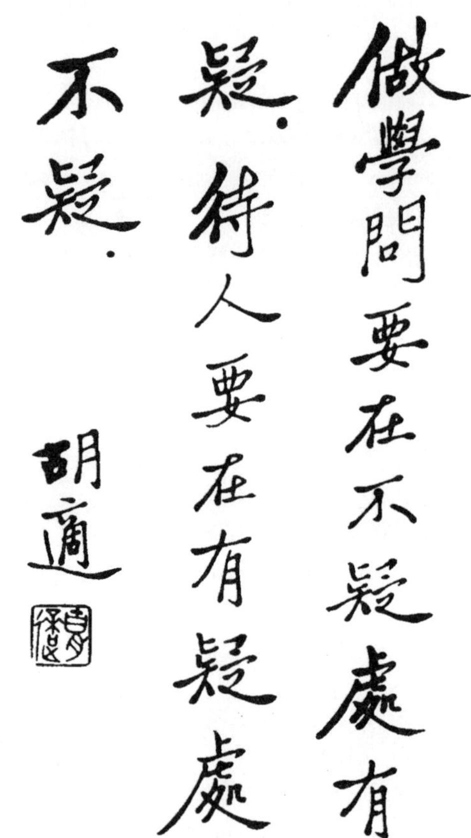

"Scholarship questions what others ignore.
Friendship ignores what others question."
Hu Shih
(1891–1962)

THIRTEEN

When Sense Differs from Original Nature

You must first love yourself and then share that love, otherwise you are selfish.

Do not selfishly covet material wealth or be jealous of another's virtue.

Do not be discouraged when corrected nor happy when praised, or you may lack the courage to change or the spirit to progress.

It is cowardice or selfishness when you avoid telling your friend his mistakes.

The above are instances when sensibility and behavior differ from our nature. Confucius and Mencius followed their nature and spoke their mind, because they knew that breaking your word injures both your nature and your senses. Every great endeavor takes into account man's innate disposition to veer away from his stated path. Advancing our culture to educate the lesser developed nations must include the teaching that reliability in word and deed instills a sense of shame. Duty lies herein, which approaches man's Tao.

XIV

The Master said, "Nearer by nature; further by habit."

Cheng Tzu said, "This statement refers to our disposition, not our original nature. Our nature is the Heavenly Principle, which itself contains no evil, and Mencius was correct in saying that our nature is entirely virtuous. Where is there any room to come 'nearer' to?"

This confusing interpretation is entirely unfounded. When Cheng Tzu equated original nature with the Heavenly Principle [rather than original nature issuing forth from the principle], he ignored Confucius' wisdom and released a torrent of misunderstanding more damaging than a flood. Mencius is also guilty for saying our nature is entirely good.

Confucius understood original nature and its virtuous makeup, and proved this when he said that neither the wise nor the foolish are willing to change. Cheng Tzu was a rebel against Confucius and Chu Hsi was wrong for agreeing with him.

(*Analects Commentary*, 17:2)

FOURTEEN

Nearer By Nature

The Master said, "Nearer by nature; further by habit." What did he mean? Since the time of Mencius and Hun-Tzu, all discussions on original nature have revolved around three basic premises: man's nature is either entirely good, entirely bad, or a mixture of the two. Most opinions were set forth with little reflection. The Sung scholars, Cheng Tzu and Chu Hsi, agreed with Mencius and said that our nature is entirely virtuous—but an original nature entirely virtuous allows no leeway for us to come nearer—we'd already be perfectly similar in nature. Mencius would be correct if this phrase were interpreted as, "We come nearer to virtue by nature, but because of habit we fall further apart."[1] But is it not contradictory to believe our nature is entirely virtuous and yet to make allowances for coming nearer to virtue? Only the sage and the fool never strive for perfection; one rests on his attainments while the other rests in ignorance. What Confucius meant is clear and obvious but no one has yet understood him. Let me give my own explanation.

In the phrase, "Nearer by nature..." nature refers to man's nature. We strive to come nearer to being more human, not toward virtue. We can follow our nature and strive toward sagacity or fall toward ignorance. Accumulating behavioral habits takes us further away from our true nature and from becoming true humans, and brings us closer to the animal world. Embrace your original nature and you begin to establish the Tao for mankind. It is our proximity to this Tao that is equidistant to our true nature.

性善第十五章

孟軻稱性善、自見孺子将入於井之喻出、而辯之者
之言皆息、不獨並世為然、後之繼軻言而起者、不可
勝數矣、可見性善如軻者、仍不乏人、惜哉軻亦未之
深思耳、人見孺子将入於井之時、性善之心、躍然萌
動、因性善之在人心、少言之、十之二三、或應有之、誰敢
說人心之中、了無性善之存在、且孺子性至純善、

Calligraphic manuscript to Chapter Fifteen

FIFTEEN

Virtuous Nature

Mencius believed our nature was entirely virtuous, expressing this in his argument known as, "The child in the well."[1] He was so convincing that since then all criticism and contrary arguments have subsided. Men with an entirely virtuous nature like Mencius will always be of value to man. Unfortunately, he never thought his theory through. Every man has, or should have, at least twenty to thirty percent virtuous potential—and it is this aspect which springs into the foreground when confronted by the scene of a helpless, innocent child fallen in a well. No man is entirely void of virtue, and those who can activate this latent virtue will not hesitate to do so to assist others in moments of extreme peril.

Lao-tzu once said, "Compare the depth of your virtue with a child's. Neither scorpion nor snake will attack it, the tiger will not maul it, nor do predatory birds claw it."[2] Do these beasts, poisonous snakes, or birds have an entirely virtuous nature? If they can activate their nature's virtue, how much more can man! Mencius' mistake was a noble one. His theories on recognizing mistakes and understanding *jen*, however, are right on the mark.

XVI

Let us interpret *chung yung* as a single noun phrase, similar to the word "taichi." Taichi is not separated with each word explained individually, neither should chung yung. However, by definition, the two are exact opposites. Taichi forms the two extremes of chung yung; chung yung is taichi's target. What do I mean? Taichi, the yin/yang symbol, manifests the change and transformation of all the myriad creatures on earth. Chung yung examines this change and attains a state of non-inclination and changelessness—it possesses the fixed principle.

To understand taichi but not chung yung is to lose the applicability of the yin/yang transformation; to understand chung yung but not taichi is to lose the steady axis. Taichi is the balance beam, chung yung is the pivot point.

(From the Introduction to Professor Cheng's *Chung Yung Commentary*)

SIXTEEN

Heaven Decrees Original Nature

The opening sentence of the *Chung Yung*, or *Doctrine of the Mean*, states, "Heaven decrees original nature; adhering to this nature is the Tao."[1] So following the Tao of original nature is man's nature; "Tao" is man's Tao. It certainly does not refer to animal's nature or their Way—heaven decrees us to be men and not animals. Becoming human requires us to follow our nature and our Tao. We must first, however, be educated in this human Tao—the true goal of all education—and then never deviate from our human realm. The Tao for establishing mankind is *jen* and duty, the prerequisites for all true men, without which we are indistinguishable from animals. Those who become animal-like divorce themselves from heaven's decree.

The word *chung yung* itself concerns man's centrality, *chung*, between heaven and earth and his appropriate reaction to the constancy, *yung*, of their forces. We can only understand the term correctly if we consider it a single, inseparable noun phrase, as it was in ancient times.[1]

XVII

Yen Hui said, "The Master excelled in leading others gradually forward. He has broadened me with his learning and restrained me with propriety."

I have read this final sentence of Yen Hui over and over, and understand that by this time his physical and mental energies were waning. Confucius once said that the process of learning is like raising a mound; if you stop digging due to laziness or other responsibilities, the project remains unfinished though it lacks but a single basketful of earth. Nature showered Yen Hui with such depth of virtue yet was so meager with years—in the end this defeated his will. How cruel and harsh nature is!

(*Analects Commentary*, 9:10)

SEVENTEEN

Skillfully Leading People Forward

"The Master excelled in leading people gradually forward."[1] Confucius led men away from evil through learning, which is more difficult than leading them by virtuous example. Yen Hui included the word "gradually" in praise of Confucius, for unless you teach a student in stages, he learns incorrectly and becomes a hermit pupil who detests his teacher. Confucius was suspicious of such unsound teaching methods. Even when the student is taught gradually, however, he may abandon his studies if no future potential is encouraged. Impatient with his perceived present situation, his learning turns corrupt. Let us be careful not to misinterpret the word "leading" as "luring." The legendary concubines, Hsi Shih and Tan Chi, lured immoral and indulgent men with their sexuality.[2]

Remember Yen Hui, who spent his short life in a humble home, content with water. His capacity for progress was unlimited and he filled each day with virtue. Confucius praised him saying, "I saw him progress, yet I never saw him rest."[3] Confucius was skilled in leading people gradually forward, yet only Yen Hui understood him.

XVIII

Atop Mt. Shou Yang, A Dream

The desolate winter landscape offers but
nettles and twigs.
Famished and weak I watch heaven's canopy fall
and twilight grow dim.
Alone I view the Western Mountains and
the pale, lonely moon.
I pass the night mourning how Po Yi
and Shu Chi died.

Cheng Man-ch'ing
(*Jade Well's Thatched Cottage Poetry*, Vol. II)

EIGHTEEN

Honor Your Duty

Tzu Lu asked if he should honor his duty without consultation. Confucius replied, "Not while your father and elder brothers are alive."[1]

Chang Tsai explained this analect saying, "Once you know your duty, perform it courageously. However, do not make any decision without first consulting your elder brother or father. Do not dishonor your duty by ignoring your position as their subordinate."

Though this interpretation initially appears valid, Confucius' answer does not explain courage but rather service to parents and king. "When your parents are alive do not travel far. But if you must travel, let it be to specific places."[2] "When at home serve your parents. Later serve your king."[3] Confucius constantly emphasized such service and always distinguished it from "courageous action." True courage, as taught by the ancients, demands reactions fast as lightning with no time for questions. It is courage that tells you to "never abandon *jen* for anyone, even your teacher."

You may possess the courage to pass through scalding water or burning fire in search of your duty, but you must accept your position as subordinate to your father and elders or you disgrace your entire family. Po Yi and Shu Ch'i performed their duty courageously when, while fleeing the court, they reined their horses[4] and rebuked King Wu for attacking King Chou without first burying his recently deceased father. These two men shouldered a great sense of duty. Chang Tsai's interpretation is totally irrelevant, for courageous action is unrelated to honoring your duty.

XIX

The Master said, "I have but one thing, and upon it I string everything else."
Tseng Tzu replied, "Oh, I see."

Confucius left and someone asked Tseng Tzu what Confucius meant. Tseng Tzu replied, "The Master's Tao consists of just loyalty and reciprocity."

Ever since childhood I've had my doubts about this analect. Confucius said his Tao was one, yet Tseng Tzu explained it as two—loyalty and reciprocity. I have heard that a minister serves his king with loyalty, and that reciprocity is the one word we could use our entire life. Moreover, Confucius himself said these two were "not far from the Tao." I have hidden my doubts deep within my breast for over fifty years. Dare I exhibit them now for all to criticize? In writing my *Analect Commentary*, I know I can no longer hide my views. I will merely set them forth and hope that, once published, I will continue to review and refine them.

Confucius' idea of a single Tao referred to the single line in the yin/yang symbol—what the *I Ching* calls the principle, the great regulator of ch'i and image. The *I Ching* even says, "With the simple and the easy, the entire world's principle may be understood." This idea of simplicity, unity, and oneness is the same principle that allows us to follow our nature and destiny. With it, we can follow the ebb and flow of the yin/yang, and entwine heaven with earth. Every single thing in the universe follows this principle. I trust future scholars will forgive my mistake.

(*Analects Commentary*, 4:15)

NINETEEN

Loyalty and Reciprocity

Confucius said that loyalty and reciprocity approach man's Tao of *jen* and duty.[1] How so? With *jen*, loyal ministers came from homes that stressed education in filial piety, which engenders loyalty. The Chinese have traditionally unified private education with government service.[2] So filial piety and loyalty come close to *jen*. As for duty, someone asked Confucius if there was a single word we could focus on our entire life. He said, "Yes! Reciprocity. Do not do unto others what you do not like them to do to you."[3] Reciprocity means to follow your heart and honor your duty, and the Chinese character for reciprocity includes the radicals "as" and "heart." So reciprocity includes duty. Pursuing loyalty that includes jen and reciprocity that enhances duty establish the Tao for mankind.

Tseng Tzu daily asked himself if he was trustworthy to others[4]—but was he loyal to himself? Tseng Tzu may historically epitomize filial piety and unflinching loyalty, and no one knows if he succeeded in bringing these ideals to bear upon his affairs with others, but loyalty centered wholly toward others that neglects personal foundational precepts is artificial. The Tao of loyalty *and* reciprocity is this foundation that establishes man.

XX

My teacher, Master Ch'ien Ming-shan (1875–1944) was a native of Yang Hu County. As a court scholar during the late Ch'ing Dynasty, he witnessed the empire's decay. When his reports to the throne went unanswered, he resigned his post and returned home. When news of the empire's collapse reached him, he nearly committed suicide. A relative asked him, "Did the Ch'ing treat you with such virtue that you must repay them with your life?" He gradually regained his composure, donned his scholar's cap, and began to teach the classics. His writings tapped into the energy of both heaven and earth; his poetry and essays surpassed Han Yu and Ou-yang Hsiu; he ably criticized both Li Po and Tu Fu. He left us but a few volumes of poetry and essays so that his ideas would be easily taught. Teachings that remain solid and reflect personal virtue such as his are rare indeed.

(*Man Jan's Three Treatises*)

TWENTY

Conscience

My teacher, Ch'ien Ming-shan, wrote a paper entitled "The Virtuous Mind," about what is commonly called conscience. In it, he makes the vital distinction that the term was first uttered by Mencius, not Confucius. Though Confucius never used this term, he did say he had never met a virtuous man,[1] which probably meant someone with this virtuous mind who followed his conscience. It is not easy to find someone who follows his conscience. Mencius exhibited just this mind together with a refined sense of duty and mature *jen* when answering the hypothetical question:

> "If King Shun's father murdered someone, would Shun protect his father or punish him?" Mencius replied, "King Shun would shoulder responsibility for his father and escape to the seashore. There he would peacefully live out his life and forget about the world."[2]

Most of the Confucian quotes my teacher used from the *Four Books* coincided with his virtuous mind. "Do not do nor desire what you should not," he would often say, "otherwise you are cruel-hearted."[3] He believed that only our virtuous mind could form a connection with King Yao or Shun, but never made a clear distinction between the two separate entities, the virtuous mind and the virtuous nature. Before he passed away he was unable to correct my treatise "The Origin of Man's Nature." Today while reading his discussions, I understood and began to weep. At last we were united.

XXI

The Neo-Confucian rationalist, Chu Hsi, believed that *Ke Wu* meant "an exhaustive study into everything knowable." But when has anyone ever exhausted the knowledge of even a single subject? If we interpret it as "eliminating excessive material desires" we equate the phrase with other similar Confucian phrases—from the *I Ching*, "Curb your desires,"—to the *Analects*, "Overcome yourself and return to propriety." Is it not strange that the idea of an exhaustive study is never mentioned in any Confucian classic, by any of the disciples? What idea is ever like a river with no origin? *Ke Wu* means simply, self-cultivation."

(Abridged explanation of *Ke Wu* from Professor Cheng's *Great Learning Commentary*)

TWENTY-ONE

Ke Wu

Every thing existing between heaven and earth is a *wu.* Man is a thing that interacts with other things. Although we believe material things ensnare us, our desire for them is always present. Foods, liquids, and sex are things specified as "The Instinctual Desires"—we need them to survive and to procreate. So interpreting *Ke Wu* as the elimination of material desires does not include our instinctual needs for food, drink, and sex. When hunger and thirst become gluttony or sexual impulse becomes debauchery—these superfluous attachments are "things" and should be eliminated. "Things" considered as both the object of man's desiring and the trap that ensnares him when excessive, differ from what pure Materialism calls "things." Knowing the difference between things and desires, we can now simplify the discussion by calling all material desires simply "things," and to strive for their elimination. Chu Hsi was mistaken in interpreting *Ke Wu* as "an exhaustive research into all things." These two words from the *Great Learning* are similar to the sentence from the *I Ching* that says, "Curb your desires!"[1] The *Great Learning* teaches us the Great Tao and was not written with the same intentions as Shen Nung's medical lexicon the *Pen Tsao* or Chang Hwa's encyclopedia *Po Wu Shih.*

XXII

Original Nature

Original nature is based on food and sex,
and does not involve good or evil.
When our desires exhibit evil tendencies,
stone statues may yet walk!
True humans differ from this,
and shun evil expressions.
Many men yet do more harm than animals,
like Chieh, Chou, and the tyrant Ch'in.
If you can strive for virtue,
goodness will sprout from evil.
Understand this single thought,
and you'll not fear death,
In life as well as death,
the sage weighs the value of all.

Cheng Man-ch'ing
(*Jade Well's Thatched Cottage Poetry*, Vol. II)

Translator's note: The above is a typical example of Confucian poetry whose goal is to educate and instill moral values.

TWENTY-TWO

The Natural Principle

What is the heavenly, or natural principle? The Han scholar Cheng Kao-mi equated this principle with man's nature. Chu Hsi agreed saying, "Our nature is just the principle. In relation to the mind it is called nature, in relation to events it is called principle." But neither understood the truth. This principle is just the natural principle regulating heaven and earth. The *I Ching* says that heaven and ch'i are above; the earth and basic substance are below. Situated between these two forces, *Ch'ien* and *K'un*, is their great foundation, man and principle. In illustrating man's Tao we can complete the Great Triad: heaven, earth, and man. Man is powerless to implement his own Tao, *jen* and duty, without understanding the principle behind heaven and earth.

All natures ride the natural principle as they originate from heaven's decree. This principle diversifies while retaining its position within the diffused, harmonious ch'i of heaven and earth. If we believe that principle *is* original nature or vice versa, we equate man's principle and nature with those intended for the myriad creatures. The common factor of principle and nature is ch'i. Nature embodies ch'i, principle applies it. Misunderstanding the natural principle endangers our human nature and prohibits us from a harmonious participation of heaven and earth. When principle and nature are both abandoned we leave the physical, natural world.

XXIII

The Master said, "There is nothing more pleasant than to learn as you constantly study."

Learning is our search for knowledge as we ponder and pursue the ancient ways; studying is the reanimation, the reinvigoration of this ancient knowledge. The *I Ching* exhorts every student to earnestly seek out the master rather than casually await the master's call.

Chu Hsi interprets the word "study" as "imitate." This viewpoint focuses on the physical aspects of learning and belittles the spirit of studying. Imitation is appropriate in reinvigorating ancient practices, but new knowledge cannot be culled through perfunctory imitation.

(*Analects Commentary*, 1:1)

TWENTY-THREE

Learn as You Constantly Study

To learn as you constantly study[1] requires a balance between acquisitiveness and dereliction.[2] It entails continuous molding and searching—like panning for gold or diving for pearls.[3] It is like scooping up water or rice: you must gingerly cup your hands, otherwise everything slips through your fingers. Below are my impressions of several classical works and what I have culled from them.

The *Book of Songs* is a monumentous compendium of numerous poets spanning several centuries. When I compare it with the epic poem *Encountering Sorrows*, I find the latter to be the work of a disillusioned man.[4] In its present form it is hopelessly tedious; a single verse would sufficiently tell its story. The rest is superfluous!

The *Analects* are Confucius' teachings recorded by his disciples. In it are such phrases as "The man of *jen* practices nothing else. Whoever despises evil must first search for compassion."

The *Book of Chuang Tzu* is the compiled reflections of Chuan Shen, composed of repetitive fantasies that ramble on endlessly. When I separate the sense from the nonsense, I find them both equally superfluous.

Today classical Chinese has been completely replaced by schooling in inferior vernacular Chinese. Students who hope to pass through life's weeding and elimination process should cultivate themselves through learning—smelt their iron to bronze and polish their jade into vessels—rather than waste their time writing. Then they will not be disappointed.

XXIV

Blood-chi refers to our body's energy,
nourished by our mother's blood.
A male child loses his baby teeth at eight,
ching-ch'i starts developing. At sixteen, this ch'i
produces sperm. Before twenty-four, his body
is still growing and this ch'i has yet to settle;
so he should restrain his sexual impulses.
At thirty-two, a man is in the prime of his life;
so he should avoid the urge to argue.
At forty, his strength begins to decline.
At forty-eight his hair turns white, signaling
the body's complete decline; so he should beware
of avarice—particularly of sex, alcohol,
and money.

(*Analects Commentary*, 16:7)

TWENTY-FOUR

Ch'i Cultivation

Confucius once said that when your blood ch'i is vigorous in youth, to avoid sex; once it matured in middle age, to avoid dispute; and when it declined in old age, to avoid material acquisition.[1] The Neo-Confucian Master from Hunan, Cheng Tzu, once remarked that where Confucius said "will," Mencius would say "ch'i." Mencius assimilated various Huang-Lao[2] cultic overtones by emphasizing ch'i cultivation, while concurrently upholding the mainstream Confucian interpretation of ch'i as the assistant of Tao and duty, man's vital nourishment.[3]

Although it appears Confucius was unacquainted with such an interpretation, this is exactly what he meant when he said that will and ch'i envelop heaven and earth.[4] Mencius' interpretation of ch'i qualifies him as a true disciple. He studied the ancients assiduously though he showed arrogance when boasting of his great ch'i. Confucius had no time for such utterances.

Hexagram #38, *K'uei*, Opposition
9 at the beginning: Remorse Disappears.

Your horse runs away. Do not chase after it, it will return.
When you see evil people, just guard against mistakes.

Commentary: The beginning 9 line does not correspond to the fourth line, the two oppose each other. There should be remorse, but because its position is correct, remorse disappears. The fourth line is the central line in the lower nuclear trigram K'an (☵), symbolizing an excited horse that runs away from the first line. Do not chase after it. The fifth line is the central line in the upper nuclear trigram Li (☲) which symbolize the eyes. They watch the excited horse and K'an, for K'an is also a thief. Li is also associated with weapons; it views the evil but refrains from attack. It just guards against mistakes.

(From Professor Cheng's *Complete I Ching*)

TWENTY-FIVE

To Love Virtue and Detest Evil

Confucius loved virtue and detested evil, saying, "Whose heart is set on goodness will do no evil."[1] He wanted us to choose and practice the good points we see in others and change their bad habits—but only as we find them within ourselves.[2] Do not take responsibility for changing others' mistakes. Lao Tzu, on the other hand, made no distinction between virtue and evil.[3] Master Ch'ien Ming-shan believed that Taoism represents the Way to survive a chaotic world, as explained by the *I Ching*, "When you see evil people, just guard against mistakes."[4] Mencius taught that man's nature is entirely virtuous and revered sage-kings Yao and Shun as perfect humans.[5] Although his theory is wrong, we see his approbation of virtue. Hsun Tzu afforded inherent evil a position as part of our nature, and we see his approbation of evil. Yang Hsiung and Kao Tzu propounded similar mistaken theories and need not be discussed.[6]

As we can see, Confucius studied only to correct his own mistakes and enrich his life; Lao Tzu was one step removed from this when he sought a method to survive a confused world and depreciated the importance of *jen*.

XXVI

Sacrificing to another's ancestor is either flattery or ignorance.

(*Analects Commentary*, 2:24)

Understanding the rites and acting upon them are two different things. Confucius assumed an acolyte's role when he entered the temple and participated in the sacrifice so as to discern the proper meaning of the ritual portrayed. This exhibited his sincerity and humility—both important aspects of any ritual.

(*Analects Commentary*, 3:15)

TWENTY-SIX

Right from Wrong

Most of the *Analects* were recorded to teach us right from wrong, but such distinctions are often confusing. For example, why is it mere flattery to sacrifice to spirits outside your own family?[1] And what is the teaching behind this: "When Confucius entered the temple he asked about every particular thing. He said, 'It is only in accordance with the rites that I do so.'"[2] True, there are many instances where knowing right and wrong is self-evident; Mencius even believed that indistinguishing right from wrong is inhuman.[3] He exhibited his understanding of Confucius' *jen* when he said:

> "Whether you prefer beef to lamb is unimportant. Once you've seen these animals alive, have no patience to see them slaughtered; when you've heard their cries, find no joy in eating their flesh."[4]

Mencius advised his students to save even a sister-in-law from drowning.[5] After Yen Hui and Tsent Tzu, Mencius was the only man to fully comprehend Confucius. Later, T'ang and Sung Confucians completely misinterpreted pivotal Confucian concepts. For example, Han Yu said in his *Investigation into the Origin of the Tao*, that Tao must involve *jen* and duty. This is clearly mistaken because *jen* and duty *are* the Tao for the establishment of mankind, there is no need to include them. Cheng Tzu and Chu Hsi of Sung times interpreted *Ke Wu* as an exhaustive study into the principle to fulfill our nature. I believe only one man after Mencius really understood right from wrong and advanced *jen* and duty. That was Lai Chu-t'ang.[6]

XXVII

Innate human nature compels a father to shield his son and a son to protect his father; though they camouflage their indiscretions, their sense of shame avoids public humiliation—correctness lies herein. It is vainglory that prompts a son to inform on his father. Petty men may consider this upright, but the noble man considers it warped. Confucius' sense of duty and principle flows forth from a wellspring deep within his breast, cleansing even men such as Chi Kung.

(*Analects Commentary*, 13:18)

TWENTY-SEVEN

Revenge Hate with Equity

Someone asked Confucius about Lao Tzu's ideal of revenging hate with virtue. He answered, "Then how do you repay virtue? No, we must revenge hate with equity, or correctness, and repay virtue with virtue."[1] Unfortunately, the word "correct" is construed subjectively to include almost everything. Common men are not sages, able to express no hate toward heaven nor man;[2] and was it not an ordinary man who revenged even an unfriendly glance?[3] However, we must maintain personal integrity to correctly surmise the equitable approach to revenge and not resort to undue violence, such as murdering an entire family. Follow your heart in search of personal correctness and adhere to this in seeking revenge. Such is the unity of words and deeds the man of *jen* exhibits.

> Chi Kung said that in his community there was a correct man. When his father picked up a wandering lamb, the son reported him to the authorities.
>
> Confucius replied, "The upright men in my community are different. If someone's father found a lamb, his son would hide him; the father would do the same for the son. Correctness lies herein!"[4]

Always follow your heart in practicing the Tao, then you will be truly fair.

XXVIII

The Difference Between *Ching* and *Ch'uan:* Maintaining Constancy and Gauging Level

Ching means constant: *ch'uan* means level. Together the two form the vernacular binomial adjective, "normal." *Ching* refers to the constancy of the Tao, while *ch'uan* gauges its movement to maintain balance. Neo-Confucianism interpreted the two synonymously, rejecting earlier Han commentaries which explained *ch'uan* as a return to constancy. For example, a righteous revolution employs the power of *ch'uan* to return to the constancy of the Tao. Chu Hsi understood the difference between the two when he said, "Just as the peculiar exigency of circumstances defines what is proper when saving a drowning sister-in-law, so to do *ching* and *ch'uan* have their own definitions." I get the feeling, though, that by not stating exactly what these differences are, he was avoiding any conflict with the standard Neo-Confucian interpretation.

(*Analects Commentary*, 9:30)

TWENTY-EIGHT

The Sage's Synchronicity

The sage embodies the virtue and power of heaven and earth[1] and so is attuned to natural phenomena.[2] Mencius praised Confucius as having a sage's synchronicity. Did he mean that Confucius exhibited the timely constancy of nature's seasons?[3]Or that he understood the synchronicity of sage-like centrality? Allow me to explain.

Confucius' remark, "The noble man is timely centered,"[4] forms the basis for Mencius' correlative understanding of the sage's synchronicity. Confucius knew when to advance or retreat, give or take, when to talk or keep silent—he was always precisely centered. Mencius later extended this idea of centrality to include the movement required to maintain a central focus, saying, "To hold to the center without gauging movement leaves you holding on to only one end."[5] Properly gauging[6] an object's movement lets you hold its center and maintain balance while moving with the object as it rises or falls, advances or retreats. This is synchronic centrality.

With his sage's centrality, Confucius could properly gauge all things. Mencius was the only man to understand this. Yen Hui understood *jen*; Tseng Tzu was filial—but both fell short of Mencius. Other men have praised Confucius, saying for example, "From the birth of our people until today, there has never been a man as complete as Confucius,"[7] and "The Master's Tao can never be reached, just as there are no stairs to heaven"[8]—but none praised him as suitably as Mencius.

XXIX

Confucius was in danger while travelling through K'uang. The Master said, "Did the death of King Wen mean that culture died too? If heaven wanted this Tao to perish, it would not be here today. If heaven wants this Tao preserved, why fear the people of K'uang?"

Chu Hsi said, "The *Records of the Historian* relates that the Grand Officer, Yang Hu, had terrorized the people of K'uang. The people mistook Confucius and his entourage for Yang Hu, and encircled them. *Wen*, literary culture, is manifestation of the Tao and another name for the rites and music. Confucius could have easily said Tao and not *wen* were it not for his own humility."

(*Analects Commentary*, 9:5)

TWENTY-NINE

Wen, Literary Culture

Confucius said, "Did the death of King Wen mean that culture (*wen*) died too?"[1] Yen Hui praised Confucius for broadening his outlook with *wen* literature[2] and Han Yu was correct in saying that literature is our best tool for teaching the Tao. Confucius showed foresight when he said that unpolished words do not travel far.[3] He himself transmitted only several thousand characters; Lao Tzu wrote a little over five thousand. Nowadays each of us, from childhood through old age, writes tens of thousands of characters. If another Ch'in Dynasty ever returns to power, the despots will once again leisurely set aflame all these writings. How much more will there be to burn when we multiply this by the billions of people spreading across hundreds of generations!

Sometimes there emerges a despot who revolts against literary culture. Like a serf who suddenly becomes a lord, he deceives the people with great audacity. He overturns established norms[4] and promulgates selfish interest; he steals a peep at the divine instruments and employs them for personal gain—for in his mind are the aggregate thoughts of a successful thief. All the while he keeps his weapons at bay. It is here that I say, "Culture does not die with death!" Remember the words of Confucius and Mencius—for slang and somniloquy benefit no one.

言何必要文第三十章

孔子曰、言之無文、行諸不遠、言何必要文、此文之一字、含義甚深、我欲澈底解之、於意有二、其試言之、一如白話者、乃方言也、一方有一方之土話、不得相通、莫說千里之遙、五里相隔、便不能解、所謂車同軌、書同文、天下一家、此非有文方能行諸遠也、一鶴鳴九皋、聲聞於天、又如呦呦鹿鳴、食野之苹、

Calligraphic manuscript to Chapter Thirty

THIRTY

Polish Your Words

Confucius said, "Unpolished words will not travel far," but why should we polish our words? The word *wen*, meaning to polish or refine, has many meanings, and so for brevity, I will discuss only two aspects.

First, vernacular Chinese contains numerous dialects. Each district speaks a distinctive dialect almost unrecognizable to most outsiders. Two persons from as far away as a thousand miles to as near as five miles may misinterpret each other when conversing in dialects. The phrase, "Construct carriage wheels uniformly; keep script styles consistent" was an ancient edict intended to unify the country.[1] Mere consistency in script, however, does not empower words to travel far.

Second, in the *Book of Songs* it is written:

> The white crane cries in the ninth marsh,
> its call is heard throughout the kingdom. [2]

And:

> "Lou-lou" the deer cries, nibbling on forest green.
> I have honored guests. "Lutes and zithers, begin!"

If animals can produce pleasant sounds, why must man utter vulgar, unrefined words? It was said: Poetry is the expression of earnest thought, singing is the prolonged utterance of that expression.[3] Harmonized and polished words move the listener and become engraved in their spleen.[4] Unfortunately, polishing your words is not a subject we can thoroughly examine in one chapter.

XXXI

**The Master said,
"When natural substance exceeds refinement, you become earthy. When refinement exceeds natural substance, you become urbane. The noble man balances his substance with refinement."**

The *I Ching* says that a great man changes like a tiger; a noble man changes like a panther—so refinement reflects your substantive character. Neither substance more refinement should predominate, and to depreciate either one or leave both unbalanced, destroys your nature. Everyone possesses the ability to change according to their character; some like a tiger, others like a panther. The noble man embraces the change; the small man ignores it.

(*Analects Commentary*, 6:16)

THIRTY-ONE

Balance Substance with Refinement

The Master said, "When natural substance exceeds refinement, you become earthy. When refinement exceeds natural substance, you become urbane."[1] Earthiness shows a lack of refinement; urbanity shows its excess. Confucius continued, saying, "The noble man balances his substance with refinement." But how do you know when the two are properly balanced? It is enough to remember that neither should predominate. The ancients believed in studying the Six Refined Arts of music, horsemanship, ritual, archery, calligraphy, and mathematics only after applying their energies toward the substantive arts of filial piety, trust, respect, love, and friendship.[2]

The Chinese character for "balance" employs a wood radical, reminiscent of the evergreen—the last tree to shed its needles when the environment turns hostile.[3] The noble man does not over-cultivate either substance or refinement. Take away his refinement and what remains looks like a shaved tiger, which is indistinguishable from the hide of a shaved dog.[4] On the other hand, the amoral man without any substantive qualities who cultivates refinement resembles a shaved dog that dons a panther's skin. This cultured scoundrel is more dangerous than a wolf. If our culture is to spread across the universe, we must emphasize substantive arts while not neglecting refinement.

XXXII

Ch'eng is the beginning and end of all things, without which nothing would exist.

The complete man does not complete merely himself, he helps others to their completion. His own self-completion shows his *jen*, his assistance to others exhibits his knowledge. He unites the Tao internally and externally and employs all things in a timely and appropriate manner.

(The *Chung Yung*, 24:25)

THIRTY-TWO

Self-Completion, *Ch'eng*

It was said that *ch'eng* is nature's Tao; self-completion is man's.[1] Heaven originates Tao; earth produces *teh*, virtue.[2] Just as earth is the foundation of heaven, so virtue is our foundation for self-completion.[3] Without completing our self we understand neither the originating Tao nor the producing Teh. Every creature on earth engages in some form of self-completion, or else nothing would exist.[4]

When you develop your nature by cultivating *ch'eng*, you follow your heavenly decreed human nature and practice the Tao for man's establishment, *jen* and duty. Afterward, you must assist other people and things to complete their nature. The complete man cultivates man's Tao through teaching; he chooses the best and holds to it, perfecting the excellence of the Way until death.[5] This process is what human nature is all about, and it is wrong to think we are born entirely virtuous. Those who understand self-completion choose the good aspects of their nature and practice them.

XXXIII

The Master said, "The people can be made to follow a course of action, but they cannot be made to understand it."

Master Cheng said, "The sage did not teach only to be misunderstood, nor could he hope that everyone understood his principles—so he just saw to it that they followed his advice. If you believe that he truly did not care if anyone understood him, earlier generations would have apprehended this apparent inconsistency. Rest assured that this was not his intent."

The *I Ching* said that all the world's principles could be understood by the simple and easy, and Confucius followed this advice. Unfortunately, the world is a very large place. Can every single person understand the sage's logic? When a compassionate government is in control, the people will follow any course of action.

It also makes sense to read this analect as: "What the people can do, they will do; what they cannot, they will be informed of."

(*Analects Commentary*, 8:9)

THIRTY-THREE

Cultivate Yourself for Universal Peace[1]

Everyone understands that it is each person's responsibility to cultivate himself, but how do we define universal peace? "Universal" refers to everyone on earth; "peace" means peace of mind. The difficulty in accomplishing this worried even sage-kings Yao and Shun. There are many self-content individuals who never worry about such affairs and live contrary to society. These recluses ignore public opinion, oppose all, and silently pass away. Let us remember that the people's will is heaven's will. We cannot ignore heaven and yet promote the people's will.

Today, the people of the United States believe they have a democracy—but in reality only a swarm of intellectuals govern. The people in a true democracy are their own masters and their will is government's guiding force. It is not where selfish men—motivated by profit—struggle to be king of the hill.[2] The ancient Chinese democrats said, "What the people can do, they will do; what thcy cannot, they will be informed of."[3] Nobody needs to wait for permission to do what is legal, and people will be notified by the authorities of what is not allowed. An example of this is when the ministers of T'ang and Wu attacked their kings and all future ministers were required to swear allegiance to the king.

Follow human feelings and you pursue heaven's will. Cultivate yourself and people will follow.

XXXIV

The Master said, "Give me a few more years and by fifty I will have studied the *I Ching* — then I will be free from any Major Faults."

Ho Yen says, "Confucius once said that at fifty he understood fate. The *I Ching* explains human nature and fate, freeing you from any major faults."

All of the Han and Sung scholars have put forth varying and opposing interpretations of this analect—differently constructed and abstruse. Chu Hsi said it should read, "Give me fifty more years…" Nobody has come to a final decisions on a definitive interpretation. Confucius taught us to be scholars amongst noblemen; to study only the essential points; to choose the best and follow it. So I have chosen Ho Yen's interpretation as the most sensible.

In the *I Ching* there are two hexagrams entitled "Major Fault" and "Minor Fault." In Major Fault, the firm line is centered but mistaken; in Minor Fault, the firm line is neither centered nor correct. Confucius thought that by fifty, his position in society would be centered; his actions, always appropriate—free from the inhibitions that a central position within mistaken circumstances had brought him.

(*Analects Commentary*, 7:16)

THIRTY-FOUR

The Faults of Confucius and Yen Hui

Confucius said, "Give me a few more years and by fifty I will have studied the *I Ching*—then I will be free from any Major Faults."[2] But did he ever free himself from minor faults? He did say, "How fortunate I am! Whenever I make a mistake someone is sure to know of it"—yet we have no record of any mistakes.[2] The ancients studied only for personal cultivation. Freeing ourselves from the shackles of habitual errors is the goal of all learning, and the *I Ching* provides the vital basis for this. Nevertheless, the other classics also furnished protection against errors: "If you have not studied the *Book of Songs* you cannot speak. If you have not studied the *Book of Rites* you cannot stand and become established."[3]

From his lifetime of teaching, Confucius gathered that our mistakes could smother us.[4] If all the teachings in the *Analects* could be summed up in a single sentence, it would be simply: "Correct your mistakes." Any mistake can be rectified when we overcome the fear of correcting it. In three thousand years, Yen Hui was the only man who never made the same mistake twice, which is why Confucius praised his love of learning.

XXXV

The Master said, "Ah, the virtue of Yen Hui. With a single bamboo dish and a single gourd cup, he lived in his low and narrow lane. Others could have endured such hardships, but none so happily as he. He was truly virtuous."

Chu Hsi said, "Yen Hui lived in poverty yet remained at peach, never allowing his low estate to shake his happiness."

Yen Hui found the joy in what Confucius enjoyed. But what was that? After reading countless volumes, I have never seen that question answered. Only Lai Chu-t'ang bragged that he knew, saying, "This idea was lost and is now found. I cannot excuse myself from revealing it." Chou Tun-yi taught his students to search where Confucius and Confucius and Yen Hui found happiness. But he never said what he thought they enjoyed. Chu Hsi said that Master Cheng quoted this passage but never answered it. I cannot spread unfounded rumors— but neither can I remain silent. *Man's happiness lies in non-desire.* Confucius said that the noble man is always composed—this is non-desire. Mencius said that self-reflection was his greatest joy—this is non-desire. He said, "Feel no shame before heaven, nor regrets before man,"—this is also non-desire.

(*Analects Commentary*, 6:9)

THIRTY-FIVE

Where Confucius and Yen Hui Found Happiness

Master Cheng quoted Lien Hsi[1] saying, "We read the classics to discover where Confucius and Yen Hui found happiness." Chu Hsi declined to offer an answer to this often asked question, citing Master Cheng's refusal to answer. Master Lai Chu-t'ang answered it saying that Confucius and Yen Hui found happiness in non-desire—a concept which the Taoist-inspired Lien Hsi certainly had in mind, regardless of his silence.

I would like to finish with the phrase "found happiness in non-desire" by adding the words "through self-cultivation." Confucius and Yen Hui studied to cultivate themselves but were unable to apply this knowledge toward universal peace—but even Kings Yao and Shun worried about this."[2] That is because these sage-kings knew the difficulties involved in bringing harmony to their subjects. By emphasizing self-cultivation, Confucius and Yen Hui could retire from public service and still preserve their inner integrity when neglected by the ruling authority. Hence I say: Cultivate yourself through non-desire.

XXXVI

Lifelong

Lao Tzu fled this dusty world
with the cry of a lonely crane.
Shih chung Confucius, however,
enjoyed this mortal realm.
A lonely moon shines lifelong
upon a field of virgin snow.
Illuminating two silent eyes
that echo ancient truths.

(*Jade Well's Thatched Cottage Poetry*, Vol II)

Translator's note: The crane is the Taoist symbol of immortality; the sun and moon symbolize a prince and minister. In the present poem, Confucius commiserates with the lonely moon, recalling his own neglect by the ruling authority.

THIRTY-SIX

Chung Yung

Chung yung is an ancient compound noun. The two words should not be interpreted separately.[1] The Han and Sung scholars never understood chung yung's main precepts and explained it inadequately. The harm these mistaken interpretations have caused is beyond description. I have analyzed their theories in my *Chung Yung Commentary*. Let me return to that work and elaborate on a few of the ideas conveyed by the word chung yung.

From Kings Yao and Shun, to Wen, Wu, Yin, and Chou, all understood that centrality was the most elusive aspect of man's mind and the heart of the Tao—none of these men ever attained chung yung.[2] Even Confucius himself had never heard nor seen any instance of someone actualizing chung yung. Yen Hui ardently strived for it, but his early death interrupted that goal. Confucius lamented on the futility of the situation when he said that a person could walk on naked blades easier than to practice chung yung.[3]

Mencius, however, said Confucius was *shih chung*.[4] *Shih chung*, synchronically-centered, is just another way of describing chung yung. From Confucius's phrase, "The complete man is easily centered,"[5] we know that our respect for Confucius over Kings Yao or Shun is well deserved. When Confucius was ignored by the rulers, he retired from public view and stored his virtue to nourish his will. Free from the political responsibilities of promoting universal peace, he nevertheless maintained influence through his centrality while teaching his Tao to his disciples. The appropriate response to the situation extended into everything he undertook.

XXXVII

The Master asked Tzu Kung, "Do you think I studied to gain my knowledge?" Tzu Kung replied, "Of course!" The Master said, "Well, I did not. I have strung everything together upon a single principle."

Previously, Confucius told Tseng Tzu this same concept, who only said, "Oh, I see." Unsure of Tseng Tzu's understanding, Confucius reiterates his concept of an all-pervasive, unifying Tao, and awaits Tzu Kung's inquiries and incertitudes—but he too falls silent.

(*Analects Commentary*, 15:2)

THIRTY-SEVEN

The Unifying Tao

Confucius said, "I have one thing, and upon it I string everything else." Tseng Tzu said, "Oh, I see." Tseng Tzu then reported this to the other disciples, interpreting the Master's Tao as consisting only of loyalty and reciprocity.[1] His choice of the word "only" shows us he deemed further inquiry into the statement as superfluous—showing *only* his unfamiliarity of Confucius' idea.

Confucius once said that loyalty and reciprocity come close to the Tao.[2] Since loyalty and reciprocity are two separate things, how can we interpret them as the one, universally connecting Tao? Confucius never instructed the uninterested nor the lazy,[3] so when Tseng Tzu professed understanding, saying, "Oh, I see," Confucius did not bother to elucidate, and his true meaning was lost. Many adults today are ambivalent about the unifying Tao; students are ignorant of the correct interpretation. Later in the *Analects*, Confucius reiterates his unifying Tao theory to Tzu Kung, who also neither understood nor inquired any further. Neither of these disciples can evade responsibility for their mistakes.

I have explained the unifying Tao in my *Analects Commentary*, where I compare Confucius' statements on change and its reliance on a unifying principle. He understood this single principle and employed it to unify everything he apprehended—tapping into the nourishing support of heaven and earth. Although my interpretation may not hit the true essence of the subject, I hope that it at least approaches the truth.

XXXVIII

**The Master said,
"You cannot understand men until you discern their words."**

Do not promote nor dismiss anyone based on words alone. We must attend to the implied meaning behind a man's words if we are to understand the man, or else he remains an enigma. Mencius' boast of his ability to discern words showed merely his sincerity to study Confucius' teachings. After finishing this final chapter of the *Analects*, those wishing to continue their study of the essence of Confucianism must begin to discern the true meaning behind men's words.

(*Analects Commentary*, 20:3)

THIRTY-EIGHT

Discerning Words

The final statement in the *Analects* is, "You cannot understand men until you discern their words."[1] Later, Mencius ventured to assume that he could discern words[2]—apparently forgetting that even King Shun found this difficult.[3] Words reflect your true self as clearly as the sun illuminates your image. Mencius' prideful boast went against his nature.[4]

Tzu Kung once advised Tzu Ch'in to show caution in his words[5] for such an appreciation is a prelude to being circumspect, an attribute of every virtuous man.[6] The character for circumspect, *jen*, is composed of the two radicals for speech and blade. K'ung An-kuo described it as reticence; Liu Ping-nan explained it as patience. I equate the word for circumspect speech with the character for wagon, which includes the blade and cart radicals. Speaking your mind is like removing the brake—but we must first discern words. The poem, "A White Jade Tablet"[7] reminds us to refine our words between mind and mouth, or else they emerge flawed. Once spoken, they cannot be retrieved to polish.

XXXIX

Divining the World I Live

Three years after my dismissal from public office,
I still found myself depressed and disenchanted.
I decided to consult the Chief Auger
and the oracle.

"Tell me Chief Auger, should I pursue a path of loyalty and truth, or follow in the wake of a corrupt generation? Should I hold my course like a thoroughbred or float atop the pond like a flapping duckling? Should I soar with the eagles or scramble for kernels on a dunghill with hens? What does the oracle suggest? The age we live in is dirty; the virtuous are swept aside while small men bellow like thunder."

The Chief Auger gathered up his divining instruments and said, "Sometimes a mile is too short and an inch too long. The answers you seek cannot be found in any oracle. Follow your heart and contemplate your actions, then you will have your answer."

(*Songs of Ch'u*, by Chu Yuan, c. 343 B.C.)

THIRTY-NINE

The Cultural Renaissance

What is culture, or *wen hua?* Confucius' and Mencius' words are refined literature, *wen*; they guide us in societal relationships and transforming, *hua*, crude customs into High Chinese ritual. So culture arises when literature is employed to transform society through education.

Noble and virtuous men have long scoffed at coarse words—writing unworthy of being placed alongside the *Book of Songs.* When the Tao of Confucius and Mencius is ignored, the virtuous are swept aside while small men bellow like thunder; our words remain vulgar and our High Chinese ritual regresses into barbarian customs![1]

Recently, Chiang Kai-shek has promoted a cultural renaissance. This requires a return to Confucian and Mencian studies with an adherence to proper familial/societal relationships—all assisted by Tao and Teh. This is a practical approach for the renaissance. Discard practicality about culture (*wen hua*), and our culture (*wen*) will be unable to educate (*hua*) anybody. We must first arouse our culture if the renaissance is to succeed.

XL

The Master said,
"Respect the young!
Their future may be greater than our present."

(*Analects*, 9:22)

FORTY

Memorization through Recitation

Children memorize classical literature by rote to remember the lessons they contain. There is no better time than childhood for memorizing, when life is free from worries and the mind possesses a great potential for learning. We must consider the child's intellectual stage and first teach them to memorize the pronunciation of words in simple poems and songs as they slowly learn penmanship, taking into account their attention span.

Many adults consider it superfluous to memorize ancient classics in this modern atomic era—but even professionals in the atomic sciences must memorize material! History provides us with a standard for the future.[1] Should we ignore our past? Can our entire history be comprehended in a single thought? Not only is vernacular Chinese too difficult to memorize, but the progress made during these past five thousand years should not be taught in so casual a medium.

I have not said everything I would liked to and can only hope the few serious students will understand the rest by themselves.

XLI

**The Master said,
"Make yourself understood."**

Chu Hsi says, "Just communicate your point, don't worry about prosaic beauty. Without clarity, nobody will understand you."

Duke Chou said, "Work on clarity, not verbosity!" Confucius followed this and said, "Make yourself understood." The former was a punitive edict; the latter was an enlightened teaching, and the two concern more than advice against glib prose. Communicating even a single word clearly has always been difficult.

(*Analects Commentary*, 15:40)

FORTY-ONE

Make Yourself Understood

Confucius said, "Make yourself understood,"[1] yet his own teachings have been obfuscated for more than two thousand years; not because his words are obtuse, but through the mistaken interpretations of later scholars. Many believe that an easy, laissez-faire approach to writing lacks depth. While in many respects this is true, it betrays shallow reflection. Consider the difference between the erudite, simple, curt *Spring and Autumn Annals*, authored by Confucius, and the other four classics; the *Book of Songs*, *I Ching*, *Book of Documents*, and *Book of Rites* [whose obtuse texts remain the subject of constant interpretation]. Chinese culture was severed in the wake of the Ch'in book burnings—those who continued research did so without any firm foundation. From Han times on, scholars devoted their energies toward creative interpretation, exhausting their self-centered intellect—their mistakes come as no surprise.

Many scholars today believe vernacular writing superior to classical literature. There are no barriers between the two modes of expression, only when and to whom we apply them. As a scholar versed in classical Chinese, if I were taught farming or carpentry in vernacular Chinese, I would not understand completely. Likewise, if I employed vernacular Chinese to teach farmers and carpenters grammatical literary devices, they would not understand. The important applications of literature, farming, or carpentry lie within our own ability to comprehend.

The unified, unbroken inheritance of the Tao is within the mind. An example of such unified teaching can be found when Yao and Shun first said, "Always condense, always unify. Hold fast the center."[2] Confucius extended this, saying, "The noble man is timely centered."[3] Mencius finally said, "To hold on to the center without gauging movement, is to hold on to only one end."[4] The Tao is passed from mind to mind. Is vernacular language an able vehicle?

FORTY-TWO

Deceitful and Argumentative

"The Custodians of the Four Cardinal Mountains proposed that King Yao's son, Tan Chu, succeed him to the throne. Yao replied, 'He is deceitful and argumentative.'"[1] The deceitful cannot be trusted; the argumentative love to quarrel.[2] Deceitful people rely on argument to confuse and dissuade—without it their deception is foolhardy and harmless. So let us put aside the question of deceit and discuss being argumentative.

From time immemorial, everybody argues when discussing right from wrong. Confucius once said that in listening to these arguments, he chooses side like anyone else—but that it would be better if no one argued.[3] All public arguments during the past two thousand years would not have occurred if the unprincipled were prohibited from disseminating their ideas.[4] Such self-evident restrictions would require only a discerning comprehension of who exactly fits into that category. The world may then usher in an age of perfect governing not experienced since T'ang and Wu times. If this is ignored and the unprincipled are allowed to voice their opinions, the deceitful and argumentative will one day assume control of the government—resulting in chaos. King Yao and Confucius were able to discern such men.

Confucius said that he did not "hold the ax handle." Holding an ax handle symbolizes the authority to dispense legal justice. Confucius was never appointed to any court,[5] for if he were, the unprincipled would never argue in defense of their deceit—and a great awe would be struck into the hearts of men. This is only possible today when virtuous men, able to discern the principle, control the government.

XLIII

Tzu Lu asked Confucius, "What is your hope?" Confucius replied, "To comfort the aged; trust my friends; and treat children tenderly."

Chu Hsi interprets this to read: "Nourish the aged with comfort; be trustworthy to friends; and tenderly embrace youth." But he is mistaken. First of all, Confucius said that filial piety does not concern merely feeding our parents, as dogs and horses are also easily fed. Second, being trustworthy to your friends places primary emphasis on yourself, when it is the aged, our friends, and children on whom we should place primary importance. To only speak of the comfort, trust, or tenderness we show is bragging, and Confucius would never boast.

Empathize with the elderly to know their needs; commiserate with your friends to gain their trust; remember your own childhood to understand the tenderness children deserve. Maintain this unity of subject with object—the disillusion of opposites.

(*Analects Commentary*, 5:25)

FORTY-THREE

Hope Versus Dreams

Great accomplishments are born from great dreams; but these dreams must engender some possibility of fruition. A Buddhist once said, "If I do not descend into hell to save souls, who will? I swear to forgo Buddhahood until hell is emptied." He also said, "When someone is ill, I too am ill. Only when all disease is eradicated shall I too be free from disease."[1] These are powerful dreams—but when will all hell be emptied? Or all disease eradicated? Fantasies of attaining Buddhahood or Taoist immortality are pipe dreams that only separate you from humanity.

The Neo-Confucians had similar dreams; they wished all men were brothers and all things their companion;[2] "The Six Classics are but footnotes to my greater self."[3] I doubt such dreams can ever be realized. We live in special times that require men of exceptional talent and vision, and Confucius' hopes may yet prove vital even today.

What were Confucius' hopes? "To comfort the aged; trust my friends; and treat children tenderly."[4] With sincerity such as this, you can commiserate with others and assist all without distinction. In reaching out to the entire universe, what could be more immediate? In taking our place amidst heaven and earth, what could be more important?

XLIV

One cannot ascend to heaven by climbing a set of stairs, yet the clouds float there naturally; the moon is certainly far away, yet man now journeys there—both are manifestations of an inherent principle. A long journey begins with the first step; the Tao is near to us all.

(*Chung Yung Commentary*, p. 27)

FORTY-FOUR

Fate and Heaven

"Fate alone decides if culture advances or perishes; individual men are of little consequence when compared to fate."[1] The Master also said, "I am finished talking! Heaven [nature] doesn't speak, yet the Four Seasons proceed and the myriad animals reproduce."[2] Confucius rarely elucidated his views on fate and heaven. Though in the *Chung Yung* he mentions our heavenly decreed original nature, he never explained original nature. Confucius rarely talked about fate, heaven, and original nature because they all lie beyond our immediate control. Mencius said it was fate that the Prince of Lu did not confide in him nor put his counsels into practice.[3]

Confucius did, however, constantly reiterate our responsibility to correct mistakes; and that the highest excellence can be attained by all. He corrected himself saying, "Give me a few more years and by fifty I will have studied the *I Ching*—then I will be free from any Major Faults."[4] As for everyone's ability for excellence, Confucius said, "The people of Hu County are difficult to teach. However, I will accept their students with no explanation for previous conduct nor any guarantee for future behavior. Why must I be so strict? If someone purifies himself to come and study from me, I receive him."[5] Also, "There should be no blame for past mistakes."[6]

Although our nature and fate originate in heaven, they differ from the nature of the myriad creatures. Man alone constitutes the great foundation of both heaven and earth. Those who would rather pity or love themselves than correct their mistakes and cultivate their nature's good aspect are certainly misguided.

XLV

Daily progress means the daily renewal of virtue. When this moral force is gathered within, you can yield up positions of authority, stand erect, and walk unaided. Practicing the ancient techniques involves learning their form, but renewing your virtue day by day and enjoying its flavor is attained only within yourself. With virtue, you need not compare yourself with ancient artists.

(*Man Jan's Three Treatises*, p. 50)

FORTY-FIVE

Progress Daily

If you can progress daily, then do so every day of your life.[1] The ancients believed that daily progress meant our daily renewal of virtue—today it is sometimes associated only with the development of better weapon systems. Lao Tzu believed that weapons brought bad luck,[2] but this is not necessarily so. The ancients taught an art of war that stressed a sense of shame; they believed that pressing untrained men into battle was tantamount to murder.[3] So every season had its form of military-like hunting tactics taught to the farmers during their free time.[4] It is certainly not bad luck to practice martial arts.

Atomic power has brought weaponry to its peak. If America and Russia began a war, both are assured of mutual destruction; this situation aptly exhibits the misfortune of weapons. A righteous war fought for self-defense should not involve mass civilian casualties—only the enemy's leader need be captured or killed. If American troops acted as true soldiers against the North Koreans or North Vietnamese, every battle would be won and their military position would be invincible. How did their military strength erode to such a degree? Because their bombs rained down upon the land, scorching every inch of earth. If American troops were instilled with justice and courage, and struck like lightning, they would be empowered with a divine strength and all enemies would submit. But they neglected their daily virtue, resulting in this carnage.

XLVI

"Within twelve months I would have accomplished something considerable" infers that Confucius would already control a flourishing country ready for such change. "Within three the government would be complete" means the government would be synthesized with education.

"Pacific negotiations must be supported with military preparedness." Confucius believed that pressing untrained men into battle was tantamount to murder, and that if a righteous man controlled the government, the people would be ready for battle in seven years. To learn from a sage for even three years would ready the people for a war they could win.

(*Analects Commentary*, 13:10)

FORTY-SIX

The Synthesis of Government with Education

Someone asked me how I'd synthesize government with education—an ancient concept widely ignored in modern times. Confucius hoped to bring about this synthesis when he said, "If I were employed, within twelve months I would have accomplished something considerable. Within three years the government would be complete."[1] He understood that rejuvenating a country and educating its people required both a country prepared for such rejuvenation and an enlightened government.[2]

> Confucius accepted the post of Minister of Crime which included the duties of Chief Minister on special occasions. At this time he supervised the arrest and execution of Shao Cheng-ling, and Lu was greatly governed.[3]
>
> Confucius remarked that empty discussions benefit nobody.[4]
>
> "I merely transmit, I do not create."[5]

Mencius followed Confucius and vigorously debated *jen* and duty—yet there was no prince with the earnest will for *jen*, so no one followed Mencius' ideas and his discussions fell upon muted ears. Confucius believed that even with an earnest ruler it would still take a generation before *jen*-like government would prevail.[6] What teaching could bring about the unification of government with education in a single generation, or thirty years? The method lies right in the *Great Learning*, the true heart of Confucius and the essence of Confucianism. Some of the ideas are:

> Attain knowledge by getting rid of desires.
>
> Virtue must be our base, material wealth is only the branch.
>
> The country must believe not that material wealth is an advantage, but that justice is the true wealth.

XLVII

Chi Tzu-ch'eng said, "A noble man is defined only by his substantive, inborn qualities. Culture or adornment does not make a noble man."

Tzu Kung replied, "I am sorry you feel that way, but as the saying goes, 'A team of four horses cannot overtake words once spoken.' Culture is as important as substance, and substance is no less important than culture. A shaved tiger or panther looks no different from a shaved dog or sheep."

Kung An-kuo said, "The patterns on the panther's or tiger's coat distinguish them from the dog or lamb. Without their coats of culture these animals look all the same."

Tzu Kung's impetuous rebuttal and his summary dispatch equating substance with culture distinguished him from Confucius' method of response. He could have spoken in a milder tone of voice saying, "A noble man's substance is seen by the pattern on his coat of culture."

(*Analects Commentary*, 12:8)

FORTY-SEVEN

Answering Advice

My friend once told me, "We should balance our desire for material wealth with a sense of cultural pride." This is certainly true—but let us not equate the two. Cultural appreciation must remain the foundation upon which we may add material possessions. The inordinate emphasis people place on material goods today makes Chiang Kai-shek's "Cultural Renaissance" ever more timely. We as a nation have ignored our own Chinese cultural heritage far too long and have failed to recognize the importance of culture or mores; therein lies the repository of lofty ideals which distinguish us from the rest of the world. We have cast our energies to the four winds in a wild chase for material possessions and have created a situation that would require several generations of education to bring back under control.

For over sixty years now classical Chinese literature has been taught to students by translating classical grammar into the vernacular. The detrimental effect of this decision in instilling cultural appreciation in children is inestimable. Are we emphasizing cultural awareness or basic substantive education when we teach the classics in the same tongue we sing folk songs in? Remember that Confucius told us that a shaved tiger looks no different from a shaved dog—it is their embellishments, their "culture" that distinguishes them from each other.

A cultural renaissance *is* our most urgent task to date. Let us not lose sight of our own cultural heritage as we gather the rich and bountiful possessions of the civilized world. Only then shall we be truly wealthy.

XLVIII

The Master said,
"You can abduct the commander of a large army but you cannot strip the simplest peasant of his opinion."

An army's strength dwells in its collective will,
a peasant's opinion lies within himself;
and any opinion snatched from him could not
have been a deeply held belief.

(*Analects Commentary*, 9:25)

FORTY-EIGHT

Make Your Will a Reality

The Chinese character for "will" explains the term as the heart/mind of a *shih*. What is a *shih?* The *I Rites* explains its hereditary attributes saying, "A scholar's (*shih*) son will always be a scholar." Elsewhere it describes an adult male; "A male son is capped at twenty, and hereafter is a man (*shih*)."[1] Confucius was a member of the government service stratum of *shih* scholars, and described himself saying, "At fifteen I had the will to study; at thirty I established myself."[2] We can know the scholar's mind by viewing his will. Will possesses such strength that it is easier to kidnap an enemy general than snatch away the will of even a common peasant; its influences are so extensive that Confucius said it permeates heaven and earth.[3] During Confucius' life, Yen Hui exhibited a lofty will; after Confucius' death, Mencius did too. The greatest will we can have is one that continues Yen Hui's and Mencius' will to emulate Confucius.

But what was Confucius' will? Simply, to comfort the elderly, trust his friends, and treat the young tenderly.[4] His will was one of empathy, commiseration, and self-cultivation toward universal peace. Kings Yao and Shun exhibited this same mind and will, but Confucius alone was given the heavenly rein to establish the Tao for mankind and to cultivate it through education. So it was said that from the birth of our nation until today, never was anyone more complete than Confucius.[5]

FORTY-NINE

Confucius

Confucius accepted the responsibility to maintain the Tao of *jen* and duty, and for two thousand years the inspired sage was the only man capable of truly practicing it. We become true humans—establishing our Tao and uniting with heaven and earth—only through *jen* and duty. This alone distinguishes us from the animals. Kings Yao and Shun promoted love, social order, maintained amiable international relations, and promulgated a dress code that reflected their governing ability.[1] Confucius honored all these while promoting *jen* and duty, elucidating education and culture, and rectifying human relationships.

Confucius said his knowledge wasn't innate but the result of assiduous study of the records of Kings Yao, Shun, Yu, T'ang, Wen, Wu, and Chou,[2] for which he was called "The Great Syncretist." For two thousand years all theories about *jen* and duty are Confucian studies.[3]

How can the average man or woman emulate Confucius' lofty teachings? It is enough if they become *ch'eng*, self-complete. Without this we are almost indistinguishable from the animals—with it we may become true humans and possess the ability for sagacity, or at least for being virtuous. Every great king was *ch'eng*—Confucius was, and Yen Hui, too. The average man or woman may think themselves as dull as Yen Hui or as muddled as Tseng Tzu—and so are no different from these true disciples. The self-complete man loves others; this is *jen*. He will not do to others what he would not like done to him; duty lies therein.

How do we become *ch'eng*? The greatest expression of being complete is your disdain for evil and enjoyment of virtue; when you treat the virtuous with virtue;[4] when you serve your parents while alive; when you serve the deceased as if they were living.[5] The culmination of *ch'eng* lies herein.

Something of Myself

When young I was poor but multi-talented—but did Confucius think a noble man needed many talents?[1] At fifty I grew my sideburns long and signed my name "Handsome Whiskers." I used my other name, Man-ch'ing, only occasionally for sentimental reasons. I suffered from tuberculosis in my twenties and now, already seventy, I call myself "the tireless old scholar." Confucius died at seventy-two, only two years older than I—which led me to write this present work. I wanted to correct the misinterpretations of Confucian ideas that arose from shallow reflection. At times I am quite scrupulous in my analysis of certain topics—such as Mencius' belief in man's virtuous nature. I do not believe such detail is superfluous. My ancestor, Cheng Kao-mi, never feared statements that appeared inappropriate; nor do I worry about my mistakes—there is always someone eager to correct me!

As a man I despise evil and consider it my personal enemy. When I was young I would assist others with no regard for personal safety. At fourteen I approached my brother's enemy in revenge and almost killed him. In the winter of that year I moved to Hangchou, and in my hatred of evil, I'd seek revenge for even a sideways glance. I would completely ignore, without regret, any friend who failed to speak the truth. I have always told people that of the Five Relationships, only friends are chosen by you; every other relation, such as to king, to son, to wife, and to brothers, is predestined. There are more people in the world than grains of sand in the Ganges, and the character of someone who chooses inappropriate friends is easily surmised. Confucius' disciple, Tzu Yu, said that correcting your friends too often pushes them away. But I believe that friends can teach you about *jen* and duty, and so I do not fear offending my true friends.

In writing these commentaries I often chide earlier scholars—but when they are wrong, what else can I do? Confucius did not act without thinking;[2] the noble man is cautious about his ignorance.[3] The Neo-Confucians believed their ignorance was knowledge, and their forced interpretations exhibit biased views. I certainly have my faults, but am unafraid to correct them—I gladly invite present-day scholars to correct my mistakes. I hope to show them the same good sense Tzu Yu showed when he questioned the validity of Confucius' statement, "Why use an ox knife to kill a chicken?"[4]

Afterword

After finishing the manuscript for *Essays on Man and Culture*, I randomly began to correct each of the forty-nine chapters. I recalled the day I first put brush to paper in this endeavor, deciding on which topics to write about. Halfway through the book, I found my intellectual vigor insufficient for the task—but there was nothing I could do but push forward.

The two main points of this book are: enjoy the ancients and earnestly seek your knowledge there; and, new knowledge is acquired by re-invigorating ancient wisdom. Confucius promoted these ideas his entire life and nobody has matched his ability to explain profound ideas in everyday language. If the student studies hard and without rest, mindful of these two ideas, in three to five years he will see new buds sprouting from old seeds, waving in a fine spring breeze.

I cannot describe the happiness I find when I study so hard I feel neither hunger nor fatigue. This joy can come to all who sincerely search for it while alone in their studies. Neglect such perseverance and all words will be empty discussions. I have long known the pain of wasting my energy on superficiality, mere bubble shadows. The pain has been etched deeply into my heart. How can I forget? How can I forget?

The Tireless Old Scholar Cheng Man-ch'ing
The Long Twilight House, New York
Winter Solstice 1972

Translator's Notes

Author's Introduction

1. *Analects*, 15:40.
2. *Analects*, 16:13.
3. *Analects*, 1:5.
4. This refers to the May Fourth Movement of 1919 which, amongst other reforms, successfully replaced literary Chinese with vernacular Chinese in school curricula.
5. See Chapter 39, "The Cultural Renaissance."
6. Classical Chinese employs no punctuation marks, vernacular Chinese borrows them entirely from Western languages. Modern Chinese literature compromises and employs the comma and the period.

Chapter 1

1. *Pa tsui* is the image of stalks rising above the field.
2. *Analects*, 7:1.
3. Ibid., 7:21.
4. The latter for his fate, the former for his ignorance of the Tao.
5. *Analects*, 14:37. During the Chou Dynasty (722–481 B.C.), the word *t'ien*, "heaven," gradually began to replace the word *shang-ti*, "Lord on High," common during the earlier Shang Dynasty (c. 1800–1100 B.C.). Etymological analysis has shown the character *t'ien* to be a man with a large head, signifying a chieftain or leader. This character was able to supply the early Chou kings with a numinous continuation from the earlier *shang-ti*, Lord on High, to whom the Shang Imperial family attributed its legitimacy. Later on, *t'ien* lost its Lord-like attributes and kept its numinous qualities, which were then applied to, and identified with, "nature." The word "heaven" should always be considered within this context.
6. *Analects*, 15:11.

Chapter 2

1. *Wen Hsuan, Collected Literary Works.*
2. *Analects*, 9:27.
3. *Analects*, 19:12.

Chapter 3

1. *Mencius*, Li Lou B:19.
2. *Analects*, 18:6.
3. *Mencius*, Kung Shan A:2. The *Chi* and *Lin* are mythical creatures that appear with the birth or emergence of a sage, or during the reign of a sage-king. I employ the term "phoenix" to emphasize the creature's mythological significance, not its symbolic representations—which differ decidedly from the phoenix of Zoroastrian origin.

Chapter 4

1. *Jen*, goodness, compassion, benevolence, love, or humanism, is the central subject of Confucianism. Until Sung times only man's application of compassion was ever discussed. In Neo-Confucianism, however, the substance of *jen* entered the debate and its substantive, generative qualities took on a universal meaning and were applied to all living things.
2. Words such as peach, *t'ao-jen*, and almond, *hsin-jen*, both have *jen* in their names. Their pits, with their spirit for life, symbolize human *jen*. The concept of seeds symbolizing a generative force behind human nature in Chinese philosophy traces its origins back to early Chinese Buddhism, which translated the Sanskrit word, *pija*, found in Yogacara School of Mahayana Buddhism as "seeds."
3. *Mencius*, Kung Shun A:8.
4. *Analects*, 4:6.
5. Ibid., 18:1.
6. Ibid., 15:34.

Chapter 5

1. The "wounding of the *lin*" is from the *Spring* and *Autumn Annals*, Duke Ai, year 14. "The phoenix is gone" is from the *Analects*, 9:8.
2. The *Great Learning*, 3:2.
3. The *Book of Songs*. Ou-yang Hsiu (1007–1072), a noted essayist and poetry scholar, offers an interesting commentary on this poem, saying, "This poem depicts King Wen who, with his fine wine, beckons forth his ministers for entertainment—much as a deer signals to others the forest grass it has found. The lute and zither were enjoyed by both King and court. For though the King maintained an austere countenance, he yet enjoyed the common pleasures." From the *Shih Pen Yi*, the *Basic Meanings of the Book of Songs*.

Chapter 7

1. *Analects*, 15:23.
2. *Mencius*, Kung Shun A:8. I follow James Legge's approach to translating *shan* variously as "goodness," "virtue," or excellence."
3. Shen Nung, the Immortal Husbandman, is the mythical figure credited with the development of farming in China. Legend says he compiled the *Pen Tsao*, a materia medica, after personally tasting hundreds of plants, poisonous or otherwise, and examining their effects on his body. Lei Kung, not to be confused with the God of Thunder, was another worthy and physician to the Yellow Emperor.

Chapter 8

1. The *Huang ti nei ching*, or *Yellow Emperor's Classic on Internal Medicine*, and the *Book of Documents*, "Counsels to Yu."
2. Literally, "The golden image clasps his mouth thrice," from the *Kung tzu chia yu*, or *Narratives of the Confucian School*, 3:1.
3. *Analects*, 10:8.
4. The stomach is part of the spleenic system. In Chinese medicine, the Five Internal Organs and their related systems are correlated

with the Five Constant Virtues. The remaining four relationships are heart/propriety; lungs/righteousness; kidneys/knowledge; liver/benevolence.

5. Chuang Tzu is famous for his dream rhapsodies; Confucius struggled with hegemonic control his entire life.

Chapter 9

1. *Analects*, 10:16 and 10:9.

Chapter 10

1. *Analects*, 5:9.
2. This is the first part of a poem ascribed to the aged living during the reign of King Yao. The remainder of the song is: "We work our fields to eat, we dig our wells to drink. Of what use to us is imperial power?"
3. From Han Yu's treatise, *Chin Hsueh Chieh.*
4. *Book of Rites*, Tan Kung A:2.
5. *Mencius*, Li Lou B:20
6. Soldiers would bridle their mouths with their chopsticks to remain silent during marches.

Chapter 11

1. See the *Chou Li*, "Officials of the King, The Imperial Chef."
2. The Five Fluid Secretions are: heart/perspiration; lungs/mucus; liver/tears; spleen/saliva; kidneys/spittle.
3. In Master Cheng's *New Method of Taichi Ch'uan Self-Cultivation*, Cheng writes, "There are three distinctions of ch'i. First, the ch'i within your body is called blood ch'i… Second is the ch'i outside your body, *k'ung* ch'i, or air. This is the ch'i you breathe and should be connected to the *tan t'ien*—the sea of ch'i, the storehouse of *ching*. Sinking this ch'i to the *tan t'ien* warms the essence *ching* which is then changed into the third form of ch'i, *yuan* ch'i. This can be absorbed throughout out entire body and permeates our bones."

Chapter 12

1. *Analects,* 10:6.
2. Ibid., 8:21.
3. Ibid., 9:26.
4. *I Ching,* "*Ta Chuan,*" B:1. According to classical literature, they allowed the upper and lower garments to hang down, while the eastern tribes in the barbarian frontier states wrapped their clothes around themselves. This is seen from the *Book of Rites,* III, 3:14, and the *Documents,* V, 24:13, and is alluded to in *Analects,* 14:18.
5. From the *Book of Rites,* "*Ju Hsin* Chapter"; and *Narratives of the Confucian School,* 1:5.
6. The *Book of Rites* defines dressing humbly or "unassumingly" as, "Not worrying how other learned men dress. Confucius dressed like a commoner, different from scholars and Grand Officers."

Chapter 14

1. *Analects,* 17:2. The Sung scholars understood the inherent contradiction of having an entirely virtuous nature and yet encouraging man to strive toward virtue, and interpreted the word "nature" as "disposition," rendering the sentence, "Closer in disposition..."

Chapter 15

1. *Mencius,* Kung Shun A:6. "If any man suddenly sees a child about to fall into a well he will feel alarm and compassion; not simply to gain favor with the child's parents, praise from the community, or to avoid the reputation as being apathetic to the situation."
2. *Tao Teh Ching,* 55.

Chapter 16

1. See Chapter 36 below.

Chapter 17

1. *Analects*, 9:10.
2. Hsi Shih was a beauty in the *Spring and Autumn Annals*, Tan Chi was concubine to a Shang King. Both epitomize seductive, destructive beauty.
3. *Analects*, 9:20.

Chapter 18

1. *Analects*, 11:21.
2. Ibid., 4:19.
3. Ibid., 9:15.
4. The *Records of the Historian*, "Biography of Po Yi." These two men epitomize the virtuous minister who retires from public life rather than soil his character and participate in an unjust government. The two died of starvation atop Mt. Shou Yang.

Chapter 19

1. In the *Analects*, 4:15, Confucius said that his Tao is one thing and upon it everything else is strung. Tseng Tzu related this to the other disciples by saying that the Master's Tao consists of loyalty and reciprocity. In Chapter 11 of the *Chung Yung*, Confucius is quoted as saying, "Loyalty and reciprocity are *not far from* the Tao." The Professor attempts to include Confucius' definition of the Tao for the establishment of mankind—*jen* and duty—with Tseng Tzu's ideas of loyalty and reciprocity..
2. See below, Chapter 46, "The Synthesis of Government with Education."
3. *Analects*, 15:23.
4. Ibid., 1:4.

Chapter 20

1. *Mencius*, Tsing Hsin A:17.
2. *Analects*, 7:25.
3. *Mencius*, Tsing Hsin A:35.

Chapter 21

1. *I Ching*, *Sun*, Hexagram #41.

Chapter 22

Note: The natural principle is symbolized as the line which divides the yin and yang in the taichi symbol. Heaven's ch'i descends with the principle and bestows the appropriate image with earth's substantive assistance. The Professor objects to equating principle with nature and instead correlates the two with their activating force, ch'i. Original nature embodies it, principle applies it. Chu Hsi equates the two by saying, "Nature is principle. Embodied within man it is his Five Eternal Virtues; in things it is their property. For instance, certain drugs have the property or principle to increase or decrease body heat. In relation to the mind, it is called nature, in relation to events it is called principle."

Chapter 23

1. *Analects*, 1:1.
2. *Mencius*, Kung Shun A:2.
3. *Hsun Tzu*, "Encouraging Study."
4. *Songs of Ch'u*, by Chu Yuan, 343–290 B.C.

Chapter 24

1. *Analects*, 16:7.
2. The Yellow Emperor, Lao Tzu cult.
3. *Mencius*, Kung Shun B:14. Mencius espoused the idea of coordinating ch'i cultivation with duty, which controls men's will, and the Tao, which embodies the natural principle. This opposed others who, under the influence of the Huang-Lao cults, were cultivating ch'i passively, that is, indifferent to external affairs.
4. *Book of Rites*.

Chapter 25

1. *Analects*, 4:4.
2. Ibid., 7:21.
3. *Tao Teh Ching*, #49.
4. *I Ching*, Hexagram #38, 9 at the beginning.
5. *Mencius*, Tang Wen King A:1.
6. Yang Hsiung (53 B.C.–18 A.D.), one of the original *ju*, "learned" Taoists, held that man's nature is a mixture of good and bad. Kao Tzu (420–350 B.C.) declared man's nature indifferent to goodness or evil.

Chapter 26

1. *Analects*, 2:24.
2. Ibid., 3:15.
3. *Mencius*, Kung Shun, A:4.
4. This was not a call toward vegetarianism but an admonition to stay out of the kitchen. *Mencius*, Liang Hui Wang A:7.
5. Chinese society discourages public public displays of affection such as hand holding. The question was then posed, "What if your sister-in-law was drowning? Would you grab her hand?" Mencius replied, "Of course. Do not confuse the rule with a particular exigency." The entire conversation was a metaphor for a drowning kingdom and the question of whether one should ignore the rites in order to save it, if that were the only way. See *Mencius*, Li Lou A:17.
6. The Professor was a great admirer of Lai Chu-t'ang (1524–1604). Lai is chiefly remembered today as the author of an extensive *I Ching* commentary unequaled for its *I Ching* mandalas and explanation of obscure hexagram transformations. The Professor made great use of Lai's *I Ching* commentary while preparing his own commentary—often quoting whole sections directly from Lai's work. He also based his *Great Learning Commentary* upon Lai's diary, unearthed in the mid-sixties.

Chapter 27

1. *Analects*, 14:36, referring the *Tao Teh Ching*, #63.
2. Ibid., 14:37.
3. *Records of the Historian*, "Fan Sui Biography."
4. *Analects*, 13:18.

Note: Revenge is inflicting punishment for injury against oneself or one's family; avenge implies righteous punishment for public wrongs. As Confucius is concerned here with familial wrongs, revenge is the appropriate word. In Chou times there were definite rules on how far one could go in taking revenge. The *Chou Rites* established an officer with the dubious title "The Reconciler," a sort of ancient Dirty Harry, who saw that no one exceeded the rites for revenge. Confucius himself confirmed the duty of blood revenge as seen from the following excerpt from the *Book of Rites*:

> Tzu Hsia asked, "What should a man do if someone murdered his parent?"
>
> Confucius replied, "The son must sleep upon a mattress of grass with his shield for a pillow; he must decline office and refuse to live under the same sky as the murderer. When he meets him in the marketplace or court, he must prepare to duel."
>
> "And what is the course for the murder of a brother?"
>
> "The surviving brother must decline work in the same state as the slayer. If he travels with his prince to the state and meets the murderer, he must not duel.""
>
> "And what of the murder of an uncle or cousin?"
>
> "In this case the nephew or cousin is not the principal. If the principal on whom the revenge occurs accepts the challenge, the nephew or cousin need only offer support."

Where the ruling authority is feeble, as it has always been in China, individuals and clans become the law, often keeping whole districts in a constant state of warfare and feudal fighting.

Chapter 28

1. From *I Ching*, hexagram #1, *Ch'ien*. The word "sage" should read "noble man."
2. Chou Tun-yi, *Penetrating the Book of Changes*, Chapter 10.
3. *I Ching*, hexagram #1, *Chi'en*. The word "time" should read "sequence."
4. *Chung Yung*, Chapter 2.
5. *Mencius*, Tsin Hsin A:26.
6. The word *ch'uan* is often placed opposite the word *ching*. The former is *movement* within constancy; the latter is *constancy* within movement.
7. *Mencius*, Kung Shun A:1. Quote of Tzu Kung.
8. *Analects*, 19:25. The word "Tao" is an interpolation.

Chapter 29

1. *Analects*, 9:5.
2. Ibid., 9:10. The word *wen* contains many shades of meaning, but the predominant inflection here leans toward "literature." It can also mean embellishment, culture, refinement, external markings, writings, and most important, the Tao that runs through all of these.
3. The *Spring and Autumn Annals*, 25th Year of Duke Hsiang.
4. Fan and T'ang were two rulers and are two Song headings in the Ta Ya section of the *Book of Songs*. Together they are taken to signify the producers of a chaotic world. The *she chi* are the "tutelary spirits of the land and crops." Literally the sentence reads, "Like the rulers Fan and T'ang, his chaotic world overthrows the spirits of the land and crops."

Chapter 30

1. *Chung Yung*, 28:4.
2. *Book of Songs*, "*Hsiao Ya*." The poem alludes to King Wen calling out to all recluse scholars. Nine is the peak of numbers, the extreme of yang. It combines the eight directions with the center

as the ninth. So nine signifies the center of the marsh, the deepest part.

3. See *Book of Documents*, "Canon of Shun," #23.
4. The spleen is considered the seat of the will.

Chapter 31

1. *Analects*, 6:16.
2. Ibid., 1:6.
3. Ibid., 9:27.
4. Ibid. 12:8.

Chapter 32

1. *Chung Yung*, 20:18. *Ch'eng* has been translated as "total realization," "realizing the heavenly principle," "truth and realization," and most commonly and mistakenly, "sincerity." It is the growth process by which we bring together all of the differing aspects of being human. This highest state of man is related to our intimacy with all things; attained either through strict Confucian learning, or by Taoist-inspired cleansing of the mind.
2. *I Ching*, *Tuan* Commentary to hexagrams *Ch'ien* and *Kun*.
3. Literally this reads, "That which assists in producing forms the basis for that which assists in originating."
4. *Chung Yung*, 25.
5. *Analects*, 8:13.

Chapter 33

1. *Analects*, 14:45.
2. *Mencius*, Kung Shun B:10.
3. *Analects*, 8:9. The traditional interpretation of this phrase is:

   "The people can be made to follow a course of action, but they cannot be made to understand it."

   In this chapter, the Professor certainly echoes Thomas Jefferson, who said: "The truth is that the mass of mankind has not been born with saddles on their backs, nor a favored few booted and spurred ready to ride them legitimately." But we must regard his assertion of this Chinese fourth century B.C. warring states philosopher being a "true democrat," as hyperbolic ethno-centrism.

Chapter 34

1. *Analects*, 7:16. The Professor follows this, the Ho Yen interpretation.
2. Ibid., 7:30.
3. Ibid., 16:13.
4. *I Ching*, "Preponderance of the Great" or "Major Fault," Hexagram #28, 6 at the top. Literally, "Wade into a stream until it covers your head." The word *kuo* means an excess, a preponderance, a fault or mistake. There is also the hexagram named "Preponderance of the Small," or "Minor Fault."

Chapter 35

1. Lien Hsi, or Chou Tun-yi, was the founder of Neo-Confucianism. He was credited with assimilating various Taoist and Buddhist concepts into Confucianism while discarding their emphasis on mysticism or illusion. He did believe in the immediacy of non-desire, as seen from Chapter 20 of his *Penetrating the Book of Changes*: "Mental unification is non-desire. Having no desires, one can be empty while tranquil." By placing the concept of self-cultivation beside no-desire, the Professor adheres to basic Confucian tenets of a goal oriented, human-activated plan toward goodness. Though this goal of non-desire is Taoist-inspired, it differs decidedly from the authentic Taoist goal that seeks the ineffable Tao; a Way beyond good and evil.
2. *Analects*, 6:28.

Chapter 36

1. In Han times *chung* was interpreted as "centrality;" *yung* was considered a homonym for "application." Master Cheng of Sung times said, "*Chung* doesn't incline to either side, it neither exceeds nor falls short; *yung* means constant."

2. There is much debate concerning the mind of man and the heart of the Tao. The Neo-Confucians differentiated the two; Wang Yang-ming equated the two—Professor Cheng neither equated nor distinguished either.
3. *Chung Yung*, 9.
4. *Mencius*, Wan Chang B:1.
5. *Chung Yung*, 20:18.

Chapter 37

1. *Analects*, 4:15.
2. *Chung Yung*, 12.
3. *Analects*, 7:8.

Chapter 38

1. *Analects*, 20:3.
2. *Mencius*, Kung Shun A:11.
3. *Book of Documents*, "Announcements of Kao Yao."
4. *Fan erh* may simply mean, "opposite to this," or it may read as it appears in *Mencius* Hui Liang Kung B:12.
5. *Analects*, 19:25.
6. Ibid., 12:3.
7. *Book of Songs*, 111, iii, Ode 11 verse 2. The poem reads:

   A flaw in a white jade tablet may be polished away.
   But nothing can be done for a flaw in speech.

   Confucius' disciple repeated this poem thrice daily and so Confucius gave the daughter of his elder brother in marriage. (*Analects*, 11:5)

Chapter 39

1. *Songs of Ch'u*, "Divining the World I Live," by Chu Yuan. Literally, the phrase reads, "The musical notes have been discarded, clay pots resound like thunder."

Note: Chiang Kai-shek declared November 10, 1966, Cultural Renaissance Day in honor of Sun Yut-sen's centennial birthday.

Meanwhile, the Cultural Revolution was sweeping the mainland.

Chapter 40

1. *Shih Chi, Records of the Historian,* "Annals of the Emperor Ch'in Shih."

Chapter 41

1. *Analects,* 15:40.
2. *Book of Documents,* "Counsels to Yu."
3. *Chung Yung,* 2.
4. *Mencius,* Tsing Hsin A:26.

Chapter 42

1. *The Records of the Historian,* "Annals of the Five Emperors."
2. *Tso Chuan,* Year 24.
3. *Great Learning,* 4.
4. *Chung Yung,* 4.
5. According to the apocryphal *Narratives of the Confucian School,* Chapter 1, Confucius did hold several legal administrative posts in his lifetime including: Chief Magistrate of Chung T'u, and later, Minister of Crime.

Chapter 43

1. The *Vimalakirti Sutra,* first brought to China during the later Han Dynasty by Kumarajiva.
2. Chang Tsai's "Western Inscription."
3. A quote of Liu Chiu-yuan, or Hsiang Shan. The "Sixth Classic" is traditionally thought of as the lost *Book of Music,* parts of which exist now only the *Records of the Historian* and in the collected writings of Hsun Tzu. In the Sung Dynasty the *Chou Li,* or *Chou Book of Rites,* became regarded as the "Sixth Classic." Hsiang Shan's basic philosophy—that of opposition to the rationalism of the age—is succinctly expressed in this quote.
4. *Analects,* 5:25.

Chapter 44

1. *Analects*, 14:38.
2. Ibid., 17:19.
3. *Mencius*, Liang Hui B:16.
4. *Analects*, 7:16.
5. Ibid., 7:28.
6. Ibid., 3:21.

Chapter 45

1. *Great Learning*, 2.
2. *Tao Teh Ching*, #31.
3. *Analects*, 13:30.
4. The *Tso Chuan*. The word *chiao*, teaching, should read *chiang*, lecture, and *wu*, military, is Cheng's interpolation.

Chapter 46

1. *Analects*, 13:10.
2. *Mencius*, Kung Shun A:1, and *Analects*, 13:5, 8, and 9.
3. The *Records of the Historian*, and *Narratives of the Confucian School.*
4. A paraphrase of the same sentence is found in the "Introduction" to the *Records of the Historian.*
5. *Analects*, 7:1.
6. Ibid., 13:12.

Chapter 48

1. *I Rites*, "Capping Ceremony."
2. *Analects*, 2:4.
3. Ibid., 9:25.
4. Ibid., 5:25.
5. *Mencius*, Kung Shun A:2.

Chapter 49

1. *I Ching*, "*Hsi Tzu Ch'uan.*"
2. *Analects*, 7:19.

3. *Mencius*, Wan Chang B:1.
4. *Great Learning*, 6.
5. *Chung Yung*, 19.

Something of Myself

1. *Analects*, 9:6.
2. Ibid., 7:27.
3. Ibid., 13:3.
4. A reference to *Analects* 17:4. Confucius and his disciples were passing through a small state. Upon hearing the sounds of the zither, Confucius mentioned that for such a *small* state to teach the *great* Tao, was like using a huge ox knife to kill a little chicken. Tzu Yu did not perceive Confucius' sarcasm and asked about the apparently wrong statement. Confucius then smiled and agreed with him. We should use an ox knife to kill a chicken and employ the Great Tao to educate men.